Best wishes

Ginny Eyster

Journey of the Heart

JOURNEY OF THE HEART

A
Loving
Family
Memoir

Virginia Hannaford Eyster

Walker & Company
New York

First published in the United States of America in 1986 by the Walker Publishing Company, Inc.

Published simultaneously in Canada by John Wiley & Sons Canada, Limited, Rexdale, Ontario

Library of Congress Cataloging-in-Publication Data

Eyster, Virginia Hannaford, 1924-
  Journey of the heart.

  Includes index.
  1. Hannaford family. 2. Eyster, Virginia, Hannaford, 1924-   3. Ohio—Biography. 4. Missouri—Biography.
I. Title.
CT274.H35E97   1986   929'.2'0973   86-13136
ISBN 0-8027-0931-1

Printed in the United States of America

10 9 8 7 6 5 4 3 2 1

*to Dick
for your limitless generosity,
and your incalculable assistance*

This is our book, Dick

*to Richie
for your caring and ultimate help*

*to Sarah
for your tender encouragement*

*to my parents
for almost writing it for me*

*to my grandparents
for the same*

*to my granddaughters
so they'll know*

The author and the publisher are grateful to the following individuals and companies for permission to use material quoted in this book:

Opening poem—The Scribner Book Companies, to quote from John Hall Wheelock's book Dear Men And Women, copyright 1966 John Hall Wheelock. Reprinted with permission of Charles Scribner's Sons.

Chapter Five—Condé Nast Publications and Vogue magazine, to quote from Elizabeth Bowen's short story "The Light in the Dark." Copyright 1950 (renewed 1978) by Condé Nast Publications, Inc.

Chapters Eight and Epilogue—Howard Nemerov, to quote from his published poetry.

Chapter Ten—Viking Penguin, Inc., to quote from Joseph Alsop's FDR: A Centenary Remembrance. Copyright 1982 by Viking Penguin, Inc.

Chapter Sixteen—"Bye Bye Blues," a song by Fred Hamm, Dave Bennett, Bert Lown, and Chancey Gray. Copyright 1925 by Irving Berlin, Inc., (now Bourne Company). Copyright renewed. International copyright secured. All rights reserved. Used by permission.

Chapter Twenty—Mrs. Vladimir Nabokov to quote from her late husband's memoir Speak Memory.

Grateful acknowledgment is made to Mr. Norman Cousins and W. W. Norton and Company to quote Mr. Cousins's comments on this book.

Permission to use registered name "Oreo cookies" and author's drawings of Oreo cookies is gratefully acknowledged from Nabisco Brands Inc.

Photographs on pages 31, 32, and 103 are courtesy of the Toledo-Lucas County Public Library.

In the quiet before cockcrow when the cricket's
Mandolin falters, when the light of the past
Falling from the high stars yet haunts the earth
And the east quickens, I think of those I love—
Dear men and women no longer with us.

And not in grief or regret merely but rather
With a love that is almost joy I think of them,
Of whom I am part, as they of me, and through whom
I am made more wholly one with the pain and the glory,
the heartbreak at the heart of things.

Dear Men & Women
John Hall Wheelock

JOURNEY OF THE HEART

Chapter 1

"She rode remarkably easily with the storms and tides, never much doubting her place or questioning her role."

—my son Richie Eyster

Her small hand was so cold. The wrist she had broken years earlier in a Christmas Eve snowstorm now revealed its poorly healed bone once hidden by the firm flesh of youth.

Resting back into the corner of the davenport in my living room, frail and pale and all but gone from me physically, my mother cheerfully prepared to die, with her mind and spirit undefeated.

The light-hearted approach to life which carried her from a big old house in Augusta, Missouri, in 1895 to my comfortable Ohio living room in 1983 sustained her well. The trip had taken her eighty-eight years.

I held her small, cold hand as I sat next to her in the stifling heat of August, 1983. The air conditioner was too cold for her now. She put her other small, cold hand over mine, and we looked at each other, blue eyes into matching blue eyes, in the way of two people who share enormous knowledge.

We had done a lot of hand holding and a lot of hand withholding in our fifty-eight year relationship as mother and daughter. Now her course had all been run, and the fears I had as a little girl filled the room.

"It can't be much longer now, Gin," she said.

"Oh, Mother," I said.

"I'm ready," she smiled.

"I'm not," I choked.

"Oh, yes, you must be, dear," she soothed. "Don't worry. Nature makes you ready. I'm not afraid . . . not at all. The only thing that upsets me is knowing that I won't see you and Martha anymore."

"Oh, Mother," I said. "You've been so brave. You have set such an example for all of us with your cheerfulness and courage."

We hugged each other and searched for words that hadn't already been said a dozen times. What hadn't we said? I was fearful that I would remember something when it was too late, fearful also that I'd forget to ask about something after the door had closed on that generation. Surely I hadn't told her I loved her often enough, rarely, in fact. So I told her I loved her again. Surely I hadn't thanked her enough, so I thanked her again.

And she told me I was so thoughtful of her and so good to her. I knew I hadn't always been so in my thoughts. I knew I had always wished for her to be less dependent on me. But we forgave and forgot as we always knew we would and yearned to comfort each other at least a few more times.

Like a double exposure, her life was superimposed on mine, and so it would be, world without end.

In 1982 Dick and I took Mother on a weekend trip, tacking our way diagonally southward through the hills of a hauntingly beautiful Ohio autumn, driving her through her final October.

None of us knew it then.

Cheerful and enthusiastic, she commented repeatedly from the backseat: "Oh, my, look at that!" "Gasp!" "Did you see that sweet little tree?" and "What's a squirrel doing out in the country?"

She never seemed to have an unspoken thought, even if it didn't make sense, and we'd laugh and so would she. "What's the moon doing in Michigan?" she once asked, and everyone laughed and so did she. Leaning on my kitchen counter one day, she commented dreamily, "You know how you spend your whole life looking . . ." "For what, Mother?" "For the perfect sugar cookie." I could not help it: I went into hysterics. And she laughed too, but her search continued.

As we drove along through the tawny countryside, I thought of how easy she was to please, how uncomplicated and narrowly focused she was. Her mind didn't scatter off in a dozen directions the way mine did. Whether it was a flowering almond in spring or two little girls growing up, she concentrated fully on what caught her fancy at the time. And for a long time it was two little girls.

She was happy that weekend. Happy to be included. Happy to be with us. Happy to be enjoying the heart-stopping beauty of another October, her eighty-seventh. In some ways it seemed as if there were a young girl in the backseat.

Mother's sunlit lake

We arrived late in the afternoon at the inn; our room overlooked a shimmering lake. She loved it! The sun was dropping low in the sky, creating shards of light which stabbed through the clouds and shone on the water. It was a picture, and she loved it.

She sat down at once at the small desk between the two big beds, positioning herself like a secretary, and wrote postcards to a dwindling list.

Later, walking down the hall of the inn to the dining room, she sashayed briskly ahead of us, her wine-colored skirt swishing back and forth, her matching blazer young and smart. The pink bow of her blouse was, as always, perfectly tied and pert.

Dick and I smiled as we watched her eager walk, but we were aware that her petite figure was growing steadily more petite.

The luxurious buffets delighted her, and she ate with enthusiasm all weekend. I only saw her eat well one more time.

At night we watched until the lake disappeared in the autumn dusk. Then we read and talked and went to bed. The three of us (Dick and I in one bed and Mother awash in the size of hers) chatted awhile in the darkness. We felt like old friends on a get-together weekend. Then Dick fell asleep, and Mother and I chatted drowsily on, comfortable and easy, feeling the closeness of the shared years.

And then we slept.

In the spring of 1983 Mother began to not feel well. She'd say, "I'm not sick, Gin, my body is just wearing out."

In May the doctor said she just needed to eat more.

In July he said "probable liver cancer."

With startling grace, she accepted the news without tears and came to live at our house.

Caring friends came and went with flowers and food and touching generosity. Grandchildren from across the country came and went with love and concern. My son Richie's fourteen-month-old toddler, Elizabeth, came from New York and kissed her great-grandmother's cheek. Mother's only granddaughter, Sarah, came from Idaho to spend the month of August, drawing her grandmother close and sharing the poignant details of her December wedding to come. They both knew Mother might never attend. And she didn't.

The thoughtful friends, sensing that Mother might not be around for Sarah's wedding festivities, brought an elegant and early (August) "high tea" shower into our living room so that mother could glimpse Sarah's future and rejoice.

I watched with a closed throat as Mother slipped off her engagement ring and gave it to Sarah, describing the sunny day so long ago that she and Daddy had shopped for it in downtown Toledo.

Three generations of tears.

My sister Martha came and went. Mother's ninety-two-year-old sister, Iona, came and went. Her nephew Roy came and went. And the summer days came and went. She smiled more and ate less. She slept well and had little real pain. She grew smaller and weaker and took more Darvon.

Stella Crosby, who had worked for us for nearly thirty years, sheltered Mother with her special brand of often-practiced kindness.

The long hot summer wouldn't quit.

On September 15 at eight A.M. I went into Mother's bedroom and as always, she smiled. I asked her if she had slept well, and again she said yes and pointed to the ceiling.

"There's something coming, Gin," she said.

I felt a chill.

"What is it?"

"Well, it's a black line coming this way. It's getting wider, and it has a number seven under it."

Pause.

"Do you suppose this is the critical moment?" she asked.

Dick came into the room, sensing a difference in the atmosphere. I sat down close to Mother on the bed and put my arm around her now skeletal shoulders.

"I don't know, Mother. Let's get up and see how you feel."

Neither she nor we could get her up.

I could tell that now she was in pain.

The slow silence of the gliding ambulance was more frightening than sirens. I tried to speak reassuringly to her through our twin pain and my fear.

In the emergency room, pain took full control.

Still. "Do you see what's written on the wall over there, Gin?" she asked. "It says 'THIS IS IT!' What do you think of that?" she said pleasantly and threw me a look of wisdom.

"There it is, floating above my head now. . . . 'THIS IS IT!' See it?"

Oh, Mother.

"There should be flowers for the centerpiece of a moment like this," she said. Then she grew thoughtful for a moment and added, "Dick has been so kind. You all . . ." Her voice trailed off.

Made more comfortable with morphine and settled in a room at last, she repeated the words she had said protectively to me all my life, "Are you awfully tired, dear?"

Oh, Mother.

The next day, when our kids called from New York and Idaho, she was still able to call them by name. A few hours later, through a fog of morphine, she said, "Tell them I loved them all." Then she smiled one last smile . . . now distorted and unfamiliar, born of one last effort to be the uncomplaining woman she had always been. Then she "slept." . . . thirty-six hours of progressively more difficult breathing as her body slowly shut down, system by system.

I cried for what there had been and what there would be no longer. And then I cried some more.

At ten P.M. on September 15 she rose up in bed, her eyes wide and questioning, and made a sound so strange, so awesome, as of someone going under for the third time. I felt I was drowning, too.

Then her long journey from Missouri ended, and her face grew young and peaceful. It was a face I'd seen before . . . one I knew so well from days long gone. No longer frightened, I laid my hand on her brow. I smoothed her dampened hair. I kissed the cool example of her smile.

She was buried in her cozy wine-colored blazer and skirt on September 19, 1983, on her eighty-eighth birthday, one day before my fifty-ninth birthday. In my mind Mother sleeps forever in a nearby cemetery in her cozy blazer, holding in her hands a nosegay of flowers from her grandchildren, and in her pocket a thank-you note from me. She always said I was the best birthday present she ever got.

Oh, Mother.

Chapter 2

Mother would have been a very happy person if she hadn't had all those children and if there hadn't been so much insanity in the family.

—My mother's sister, at age ninety-one, in 1982, describing her mother

My aunt and my mother both looked surprised when I burst out laughing at my aunt's description of her mother. Then they both smiled rather tentatively. I could feel their minds slipping briefly back into dark places where I could never go.

On a summer day in 1982 I was spending the afternoon with my mother (then age eighty-six) and her sister (age ninety-one), urging them to talk to me about their early life. And they did. They talked of life as it was for them, growing up in Missouri and Ohio before, during, and after the century's turn. It was a wonderful day for listening.

After a warmup of twice-told tales, they suddenly broke through into new territory. Spurred on by the presence of a serious listener, they spoke with eagerness and keen recollection. They spoke of the dear, dead days not beyond recall. They talked of mud streets in Missouri and streetcar rides in Toledo on the Long Belt car, of surrey rides for berry-picking on Ginger Hill, of inter-urban trips to Toledo Beach and taffy pulls on Twenty-first Street, of baffling illness and sudden death, of homemade clothes and sleigh rides on Franklin Avenue. They spoke of simple joy and complex sorrow.

The living room of my aunt's home filled with words and late afternoon sunlight as the two elderly sisters returned together to their childhood for an afternoon.

Two elderly sisters

Let me ask you something. . . .

Does every family have a rakish uncle, an uncle whose plans never seem to work out? Who talks of wild, foolproof schemes, who collects first editions and Caruso records? Who wears orange, pointy-toed shoes and whose life ends in the Maumee River?

Does every family have a brilliant maiden aunt who teaches Shakespeare and who goes to Europe for The League of Nations, who has a Quaker turn of mind and an art studio in Philadelphia . . . and who disappears for forty years?

Or, how about a great-grandfather who is murdered for tying up a stray cow at the corner of Wakeman (now Vermont) and Bancroft streets in Toledo?

Or another great-grandfather who desperately switches caps with a rebel soldier, escapes from Andersonville Prison during an exchange of blue-and-gray prisoners, and returns north with tales of Georgia's red water and black bread?

Or a dapper maternal grandfather who swashbuckles around little Augusta, Missouri, as mayor, railroad telegrapher, and local pugilist, agile, quick-witted, and ill-fated, whose little daughter, Iona, watches frozen as a train passes over him. Whom fate saves for a slower and more painful death at forty-five (after ten years in "the insane asylum out on South Street" in Toledo)?

Are you still there?

After my talk with Mother and her sister, I became aware again of time's hand on my shoulder.

At last I went up to our attic and brought down grandfather's box.

Over the years, whenever I hauled Christmas ornaments out of the attic, a compelling ritual brought me to my knees in front of Grandfather's box of genealogy. I riffled silently through pages of family trees, intriguing old photos, quaint-sounding names (Jabez and Phoebe) and phrases ("died of mortification"). All this had lain mute in his box for forty years or more.

Underneath grandfather's imprisoned personality there had been a searching intellect. But, to my dismay, his papers now seemed as dry

Mother in homemade clothes; red coat with monkey fur!

and dull as grandfather himself. He had left out all the fascinating details. Thus, all our ancestors were lost to us. We were to know them in name only.

So I am determined, as I get ready to be an ancestor, to make my relatives come alive for my children. I want them to be able, if they choose, to understand something of the touching mistakes, the exhilarating moments, the bruising hours, the piled-up wisdom and skill which matured their immediate ancestors—those friendly ghosts who stand in an unending line behind their lives.

This is a gift to my children, even though they don't even know they want it—yet.

Chapter 3

If you treat people right when they're alive, you won't have to go to the cemetery so much.

—My father

My first clear memory is an indelible cameo, very early and redolent with tender fragrance.

I am lying in a white crib with screening around and above me. I can reach and touch the screen.

I am very small, younger than three. It is summer. A small, open window above my bed is letting soft air and light into my naptime. The screened-in baby bed I am lying in is a popular one, called a Kiddie Koop. It is in the northeast corner of my mother's Coty-scented bedroom. It is here that I begin to look out and see the world as a positive place.

The fragrant room with the flowered wallpaper is on the second floor of a new six-room yellow-clapboard Dutch Colonial-style house.

The house has dark green shutters and a small, tidy front yard. A sidewalk divides the yard, and four steps lead up to the front porch. The house is in the middle of a row of six houses on a block. The neighborhood is young and middle class in one of the geometric new suburbs which are pushing the edges of Toledo toward the sunset. Flat Ohio farmland lies a few blocks west and north.

It is 1926 or 1927. There is a feeling of everything beginning. The houses, the trees, the flowers, the children, all of these are starting out together.

I can see every detail of my mother's bedroom in my mind, though I have not seen it once in forty years. I loved that room. It always seemed as if it were my mother's room, although my parents shared it. As I grew up and slowly moved away from there, out into the dumbfounding world, I left pieces of myself back in that room.

I am sure it was my mother who chose the small rectangular rugs which were scattered about the floor. They were "Roaring Twenties" orchid in color, with two-inch green borders. Hung too high on the wall near the open window near my bed was a framed picture cut from a magazine of orchid tulips in a white wicker basket.

Every room seemed to have a lovely picture (often of children who mother thought resembled Martha or me), cut from a magazine, framed and telling. Paintings by Daddy's many artist friends were here and there, but all of Daddy's fine paintings and pastel portraits were restricted to our basement recreation room. I used to wonder why. Mother said it was because the recreation room was like Daddy's studio.

As I grew older, the most important thing in Mother's room was a large wicker armchair, painted green with orchid cotton cushions. It stood next to the window facing south and overlooking the driveway which ran between our house and our neighbors the Lennexes.

It was in the wicker chair that I read *The Bobbsey Twins* and *Pollyanna* and *Robinson Crusoe*. Here also I fell in love first with Honeybunch and finally with Ashley Wilkes. Here I first learned the awesome addicting power of language from Charles Dickens and Victor Hugo while reading *David Copperfield* and *Les Miserables* on the short winter afternoons after school. In that same wicker chair I read *Gone With The Wind* in the summer of 1936, when I was eleven, and felt the first stirring wonder at the mysterious vibrations between Scarlett and Rhett. I felt, however, no particular curiosity when I read the line, "Rhett's lips traveled to where Scarlett's kimono fell open." I knew of course he was kissing her shoulder.

Up in Mother's room, alone in my wicker retreat, I was soon deeply into movie magazines. As adolescence advanced, I became an incurable romantic under the twin influences of the Brontes and Metro-Goldwyn-Mayer. As an awakening devotee of romance, I mooned over Heathcliff (Laurence Olivier) and Armand (Robert Taylor) with equal fervor and with a complete lack of discrimination. (Heathcliff and Laurence, however, to my great credit, were the ones who took up permanent residence in my psyche.) Unrequited and/or thwarted love, those oldtime favorites, became my favorites too. Comedy had its place, but for a thirteen-year-old nothing compared to Heathcliff's immortal crying out for Cathy over the windblown English moors.

In that reclusive corner of my mother's room I malingered like Heathcliff, staring out into that neighborhood full of normalcy and kids and dogs and decent people, dreaming out the window, absorbing the seasons that were changing as slowly and swiftly as I was. Here the moodiness and radiance of the seasons took a firm and influential hold on me.

Though Daddy and Mother shared the bedroom, evidences of him were slim. His meagre 1920s wardrobe, which included spats, took up limited space in the small closet which they shared.

I liked when I was small to go into that closet with its little window and stand among the folds of Mother's pale aqua taffeta evening gown which rustled among the dresses of her also limited wardrobe. I liked to nuzzle in the leftover fragrance. Despite the Depression, the pale blue party dress, with the giant bustle-type bow in back, was a clear sign that there were good times to be had.

In those early days, I was conscious of the lingering romance of my parents' courtship. Mother spoke often of how she and Daddy had met at a dance at the old Coliseum at Ashland and Bancroft here in Toledo. That charismatic guy, Mark Hannaford, had just returned from serving in France in World War I and was still in uniform. It was

"That charismatic guy, Mark Hannaford . . ."

Daddy at
Camp Beauregard

the spring of 1920, and love was in the air. (Mark had remained in Europe after the armistice at the University of London to continue his art education.)

Mother came to the Coliseum that night in a blue pleated skirt and a black sweater, accompanied by her chaperoning Aunt Millie. Mark saw Mother walking across the dance floor, and he was attracted by her carefree grace and her pretty legs. He was soon to be captivated by her guileless disposition. He commented about Mother to his wartime buddy, Bob Lowry, and with exquisite timing, Bob gave Mark a friendly shove. With the help of that shove, Mother and Daddy danced liltingly into the future to the tune of "Three O'Clock in the Morning."

Mother claimed that they danced together that night "like we'd been trained," and she fell asleep nightly for months thereafter humming "their song." They never really did stop humming that tune.

Despite other suitors, Mother fell in love, and six months later my parents were married in The First Congregational Church on Collingwood Boulevard on a golden October afternoon in 1920.

Engagement Day

Mother used to say that, even after my sister Martha was born in 1922 (two years before I was), she and Daddy were still given to parking and spooning in the Jewett, which Daddy's parents had given him when he returned from the war. In 1983, at age eighty-seven, in the final tenth of her life, she continued to resist the vicissitudes which befell her peers, Mother didn't appear to fear the bell tolling for her as I did. She retained much of the guileless quality that, as a young girl striding buoyantly across that ballroom floor, first caught my father's artist's eye.

Physically, I passed her a long time ago (I feel it when I bend to hug her ninety-pound frame), and I passed her emotionally the day we changed places with her question, "Do I have to wear boots today?"

When I hold her fragile frame in a hello or good-bye embrace, I am startled by her diminishing circumference, by the overlapping of my arms. Old problems and regrets melt away, and I am momentarily blinded by the intruding memory of her youthful strength and tenderness guiding and comforting me down the years.

*O*ur house was full of dozens of simple and inventive applications from my father's creative mind. His inventive stamp was in every room and spilled down the basement stairs, out into the garage and over into the backyard.

Because my childhood was dotted with periodic bouts of asthma brought on by cold and mold, my father created a special nightlight in the upstairs hall ceiling. Pulling on a string, which hung from the light in a long oval, dimmed or brightened the orange light bulb. In those days no one ever heard of a rheostat. I thought my father was making magic for me. Only on the nights when I was having trouble breathing did the orange glow soften the darkness. It was really my father's concern for my comfort that lit those nights.

Often on those same nights my mother would sit up in bed, leaning against the unyielding metal rungs on the headboard, humming and dozing and holding me upright against her chest to ease my breathing. There was little medicine to help in those days. She was not the first mother to hold a sick child in the darkness, but it was then that I learned the sweet lengths to which parents would go to smooth the way for their children. I always felt cherished.

On a small nighttable by the bed in my mother's room stood a Lady Lamp, about twelve inches high and made of wire and organdy. I guess that the Lady Lamp was in vogue at that time, because my friend Julia's mother had one in her room too. I've never seen one since.

The lady intrigued me. She wore a hoop-skirted lavender gown with tier upon tier of organdy ruffles over a wire frame. Under her voluminous skirt she wore . . . a light bulb. Sometimes as a treat, Mother would put me to bed in her bed, and I would fall asleep beside the lavender light of the Lady Lamp. The delicious mystery of that glow caused me to sleepily and repeatedly lift her skirt and repeatedly be startled by the stark mechanics beneath the feminine haute couture.

I remember occasional other nights in that room, when I was four or five and fantasy was still reality for me. One stifling summer evening I was in my parents' bed, which had been placed in a new position by the open front window to catch whatever night breeze might stir. Mother told me that the sandman would be coming soon. After she left the room, I studied the window screen, wondering how the sandman could filter through that tiny network of wire. I never questioned that he was out there, though, floating like a dusty Peter Pan in the twilight, friendly and helpful, waiting to scatter sand and lead tardy little sleepers to dreamland.

Chapter 4

I feel like a music box with the music all shut inside.

—Helen Keller

In my bedroom, especially on cold and absolute winter nights, I would listen to the haunting sound of a distant train whistle. . . . It is the same whistle that everyone seems to have floating in his memory. I imagined that the tramps we so often heard about then were huddled in boxcars, cold and hungry.

It was here at night in my room that I worried about my parents dying; where I sang in the darkness the popular songs of the day; where I wondered vaguely about God and relived the days as they accumulated.

It was here that I cried as I listened to the sounds of celebration below. It was a party for my father's fortieth birthday, and I knew that he was growing old, . . . that it was the beginning of the end for him. It was the unthinkable thought, . . . as Wordsworth said, the thought "that lies too deep for tears." But I cried.

I didn't know that the dreams that I dreamed in my bedroom would be so long in coming of age.

In that same room I tossed for many hours in delicious anticipation on at least a dozen Christmas Eves. All children whose families celebrated Christmas were doomed to helpless and tormented wakefulness on this most precious evening of the year. It was a luscious anxiety, and I remember the feeling of loss on the first Christmas Eve when I fell asleep effortlessly. I knew childhood was losing its magic hold on me.

Daddy's talented, pretty, deaf sister Albertha (named for her father Albert) came to sleep at our house every Christmas Eve to share in the early Christmas morning enchantment that children bring to that day. It was a joy she should have been allowed to experience through children of her own, but her parents, while loving her dearly, prevented her marrying. They felt they were sparing her further heartaches lest she have deaf children of her own. The chances were good that they were mistaken. (And even if they were to have married and had deaf children, I know her life would have been deeply enriched, and theirs too!)

And so, the well-intentioned great mistakes are made.

Daddy's talented, deaf sister

For twelve years she attended the Ohio State School for the Deaf in Columbus. As her talents and her loveliness grew, so did her suitors. They too were deaf, and her parents were afraid.

Albertha was later offered a teaching position at the school she had attended, but another well-intentioned mistake was made. Her parents decided she should now be at home.

It moves me even now when I think of the lonely decades she need never have endured. Albertha, a younger version of her devoted mother (my paternal grandmother Julia), was deeply dependent (despite her years away at school) and attached to the animated and caring woman who was her world. At her mother's, knee she learned to knit and embroider and crochet and paint and quilt and accept her fate.

Her natural talent was encouraged with extended study, and she even had her own kiln in the basement of her home on Rosalind Place. The kiln was bought to enable her to fire the china she had so delicately decorated. She filled many orders for family and friends.

My life and my home today are filled with quilts and tablecloths, afghans and teapots, samplers and dishes that she and her mother stitched and knitted and embroidered and painted. As I write, I have only to look ahead, behind, or beside me to enjoy the heirlooms they left behind.

But the obscurity of their inner lives frustrates me. Their interior world, their ways of dealing with life's complexities, can only be guessed at by their rather lighthearted and jocular way of bantering. Only Grandpa showed no mirth, but even he had a droll sense of humor.

No diaries or confessional journals remain, however.

But the outpouring of their hands filled all the extra moments of their lives with handiwork of startling power and invention.

I need to thank Albertha this morning, . . . not so much for the many reminders of her life which surround me, but for the example of her consistent good nature. Her cheerful manner, whether real or assumed, flew in the face of the appalling loneliness of her deafness. (It is uncertain, but probable, that she became deaf after severe scarlet fever when she was a toddler.)

I also need to tell her that I am sorry that my sister and I, her only youthful relatives, seemed too busy with our own growing up to share with her the time her life deserved. This fact is at the very top of my list of regrets.

Albertha was not overlooked when laughter swept the family circle. Because she could lip-read, she was able, with natural wit, to follow the conversation back and forth across the room. Once in awhile the exchange would get away from her, and her face would cloud over. Perched lightly on the arm of a chair, she would look expectantly at each of us, her light, lively eyes sweeping over each mouth for clues. Then, in the next moment, she would be laughing with us.

I read once that Helen Keller said she felt like a music box with the music all shut inside. I wonder if Albertha felt that way too. I wonder if she might have wanted to sing like Daddy, but found her voice trapped inside.

An overnight picnic for the deaf at Cedar Point, Sandusky, Ohio. Albertha in white hat in front of tree. Grandmother in front row with huge hat (child on her lap unknown). Daddy in front row (boy holding doughnut on extended finger). Daddy spoke of picnic's eerie silence after darkness fell.

As much as she was able, she resisted the use of sign language, because she wanted to become expert at lipreading. She did not like the attention that signing attracted in public, so Martha and I were taught very little of it. But at home Daddy, Grandpa, and Albertha resorted frequently to it. I remember watching, especially on Sunday afternoons, as the graceful, silent gestures crisscrossed the Victorian parlor. Grandpa especially had learned to sign quickly. I remember he

A Christmas calendar from Albertha to her parents, 1901

could sign words consecutively on each hand to speed up his communication with Albertha.

I can see Albertha now, small, slim and pretty, with dark-lashed, sky-blue eyes, . . . arresting eyes, . . . eyes that seemed to be seeing things the rest of us did not see. She is circling Grandmother's ornate parlor in my father's arms. She is ten years his senior. She is laughing as she and Daddy dance to the tune which my father is humming. Which she can feel but only we can hear.

They danced together frequently in graceful Sunday afternoon circles, while Martha and I watched and shot paperwads from taut rubber bands into the parlor's hanging chandelier.

As children, we were totally unaware of the ongoing anxiety which underlay the light behavior of the adults . . . anxiety over the erratic and ominous behavior of Uncle Bobby. (More about him later.)

I did not realize it at the time, but my grandparents' home and their life-style enabled me to observe firsthand the mores and artifacts of the vanishing Victorian era, that ice age of human emotions, where hypocrisy was encouraged and reality repressed. My parents were then to become part of the great Victorian thaw in the Roaring Twenties when the old restrictions broke apart. Theirs was not the style of the Jazz Age, but it was a departure from the preceding era.

I am glad that I can return in my mind's eye, whenever I please, to that familiar, controlled home with its gentility and touches of gingerbread. Mostly, I like to return to the warm, aromatic kitchen with the steamed-up windows, the huge black iron stove, the pump on the sink, the wooden icebox on the cold little back porch, and the purposeful women, their cheeks flushed with holiday effort.

My grandmother Julia died in October, 1939, after a heart attack following an escapade by Daddy's older brother, my Uncle Bobby. Grandfather's decline accelerated after her death, and he only lived till spring.

His mind left us long before he did. He began to wear his hat to meals; to drink from the cream pitcher; to tease our also senile dog; to prowl the house endlessly; to lock himself in his bedroom and then quickly lean out the window and shout to the neighbors, "They've locked me in again!" Funny now, not then.

When Albertha's parents died, the protected, restricted world with which they had surrounded her went with them. She was devastated by the loss of her mother and lay across her body, refusing at first to let her go. Grandmother had been her little daughter's loving link to the hearing world. It was a world Albertha entered primarily through her mother. Now she was to be alone in the silence.

Mother and Daddy didn't quite let that happen.

Finally, in 1950 Albertha moved to Florida with my parents, who retired to Clearwater when they were only in their mid-fifties. She died there of cancer in 1953 at the age of sixty-nine, cared for by my parents and cheerful to the end. One day shortly before she died, as my mother bathed and dressed her, Albertha, frail and smiling, said, "Ed-e-na . . . I am your doll."

Chapter 5

Christmas is like a note struck on glass—long ago and forever. . . . we celebrate, dazzled and drawn together; somehow more than ourselves. Who, what has joined our company?

—Elizabeth Bowen

Back now to Christmas Past.

On that twinkling morning of mornings for children, Martha and I were not allowed to go downstairs until Aunt Albertha was ready to go down too. We sat together, happy and eager on the top step, unable to see what awaited us downstairs, looking impatiently over our shoulders to the bathroom where Albertha was going through her morning ritual of combing and washing, just as if it were an ordinary morning.

We edged down a few steps as the multicolored sparkle of the Christmas tree climbed the stairway to lure us into disobedience. We never did go down without her, though. Somehow, even as very small children, we were able to realize or understand the need to include Albertha in our delight on this day.

Even though money was hard to come by, parents usually managed to somehow make Christmas special for their children. One important Christmas Daddy built us a wonderful doll house which was a rough replica of our own house. And Mother copied interior details down to the wallpaper and little rugs.

Baby dolls with ruffled bonnets, Nancy dolls, Margie dolls, Patsy dolls, Dorothy, and my English doll, Pat, march through my memory in a sweet parade. Their pensive little faces are clear to me, their blue eyes still wide and unblinking.

There were little trunks filled with doll clothes that Mother made in tiny duplication of our own dresses. And we had one magical and

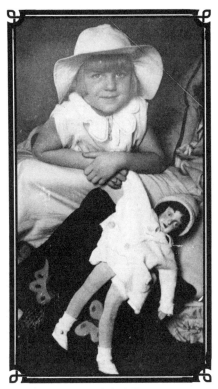

My English doll, Pat

marvelous doll. She was the size of a year-old child, with a three-inch tin-lined hole in her tummy. In the middle of her cloth back was a little implanted record player with tiny blue cylinder-type records. Here we placed little records of lullabies and nursery rhymes. We cranked the handle that projected from her side and listened to the muffled tunes waft from her tummy and through the folds of her baby dresses.

We called her "Subscripsy" because she had been won by my father in a contest at *The Blade/Times* for getting people to subscribe to the paper. Later we tried to change her name to Barbara, but it was too late. Subscripsy it was.

After the gifts were opened on Christmas morning, Daddy's parents arrived to have Christmas dinner with us. I remember Daddy's mother, Julia, as she was on a particular Christmas morning when I was eight or nine years old. The air was full of cold sun and excitement and a few errant snowflakes. Grandmother swept in on a rush of frosty air and in a swirl of mink—confident, beautiful and bountiful—her blue eyes dominating her lively face. Her regal bearing gave the impression that she was much taller than her five-foot-two frame indicated. Her cheeks were flushed, and unmelted snowflakes rested on her coat sleeves. She carried a large willow basket, full of Christmas over her arm. It was then I realized for the first time that she was not just a grandmother but a beautiful woman too.

My grandmother, Julia Heck Hannaford

Grandfather (Albert Swan Hannaford), born and bred in New England of English ancestry, followed behind her, a remote, private gentleman whose humor lay hidden in his quiet places. It erupted dryly now and then, but he did not relate to children and paid little attention to Martha and me. We never really knew him at all. We sized him up from a careful distance, checking out his high black shoes.

Apparently Grandmother wasn't just lovely to behold, but she was blessed with a generous spirit and a lively humor. Even my mother, who has been known to pick up on a fault, admired her unreservedly. Today Mother still speaks generously about her mother-in-law, about her giving nature (how she would often furtively tuck money down the neck of Mother's dress or blouse), and about her loving acceptance of those around her. She tells also of the pain Grandmother experienced over her little daughter's deafness, and the sorrow she felt when people took notice.

I feel cheated when I reflect that I inherited so little of Grandmother's beauty. I regret that the purity of her patrician face couldn't have passed down undiluted . . . that the less delicate family features couldn't have been recessive.

If nothing else, my middle name is Julia. As a child, given the inexplicable reasoning of childhood, I decided I didn't like the name Julia combined with Virginia. Years later when I married, I even omitted Julia on the wedding invitation. I regret that my parents allowed that youthful whim to prevail. Although it wasn't a big thing, I am glad that my grandmother wasn't alive and never knew of that small slight perpetrated by a thoughtless granddaughter. But Albertha knew. Albertha Julia.

The Christmas dinner table that year was set with the usual white linen cloth. In the center was a red brick chimney made by my father from a cardboard box. The box was covered with red brick paper, and the edges of the chimney top dripped cotton snow. Red streamers led from the chimney's secret depth to each person's place. So each one received a small gift when the streamer was tugged.

My grandparents gave me a beautiful powder-blue coat that year, with a long row of buttons like ivory marbles down the front. Running down the outside edges of the sleeves was a wavy, Indianlike design in white angora. This lovely coat with a white beret is the only gift I remember receiving from my grandparents, although I'm sure there were many down the years.

As that Christmas day wound down and the corners of the room began to fill with dusk, the family, including Uncle Bobby, took their places around the Atwater-Kent radio to listen to Lionel Barrymore in his annual portrayal of Scrooge in Dickens's "Christmas Carol." Uncle

Bobby sat restlessly on the piano bench, wiggling his feet, constantly shifting his position, eager to get on to the next thing.

After Tiny Tim's "God bless us, every one!" we all sat back down around the dining room table. The blue snow-light beyond the windows and the rising wind pushing to get in intensified the feeling of warmth inside.

Mother sat at the table, relaxing, her left hand resting in a familiar position at her throat, her fingertips tucked under the ruffle of her collar. Daddy cracked walnuts and jokes with his usual flair. Martha and I, feeling the contentment, were quieter than usual. Grand-mother looked around the table at her family, tenderness in her eyes. We ate cold turkey and warm fruitcake and walnuts and held onto the day as long as we could.

Candlelight cast small shadows on the faces of the eight family members around the table. Grandma and Grandpa, now growing old with their hair white, sit with their two look-alike, act-different sons; their pretty, handicapped daughter; their one pleasant daughter-in-law; and their two energetic granddaughters momentarily stilled.

Light from the Christmas tree in the darkened living room spilled over the mellow scene. There were pauses, moments of silence, and the sacred sense of something at the center of our celebration.

The conversation bubbled and faded as peace and goodwill and fatigue settled over us and the houses on our block. Christmas darkness enfolded the neighborhood.

The day slipped rich and tinseled into my cache of perfect memories.

Julia's house at 126 Rosalind Place, Toledo, 1902. Grandmother Julia is second from left and Albertha on the far right.

Chapter 6

We two kept house,
The past and I.

—Thomas Hardy

Back in those days when time was roomy and endless, we kids lived in a reassuring world. We were perhaps the last of the lucky ones before technology blew apart the snug, secure edges.

We thought nearly everybody was good, at least the middle-class group that I grew up with did. We knew there were bad people, but they always seemed to be someplace else. We knew about gangsters, but they were part of an underworld from which we felt removed. We were not assaulted by the turbulent, traumatic portrayals of crime and war which were to invade our future homes and the psyches of our children via television.

Those days, those rooms, that house where I grew up. It all seemed so uncluttered, so stylized and nostalgic. That's it. Stylized, like the art deco of the period. The clean, simple lines, in reaction to Victorian geegaws. Outside our house, the world was predictable and comprehensible and within our grasp, or so it seemed.

There was something about the texture of childhood days in the thirties that has left an unconscious yearning in all of us who lived them. Everything was in its proper place. People knew what to expect. There were no blurred edges.

Summer always came. And it brought lots of things to the neighborhood besides spirea and lilac. The daily sound of horses' hooves bringing all manner of goods to our doorsteps was so reassuring. And the horses brought manure to the streets for the neighborhood dogs to roll in. This kept the mothers occupied.

I remember the mournful, singsong call of the junkman, clattering by in a rickety wooden wagon that seemed to befit his function. He also blew a horn that made a sound like a wounded elephant. So between singing and honking and squeaking and rattling, we knew our deliverance from junk was at hand. I can see him yet. He's down at the corner, his wagon creaking along our tree-lined street, leaving a dusty wake behind, temporarily blocking out the sun.

Most things came to our neighborhood by horse and wagon.

And there was, of course, the cool appeal of the no-nonsense iceman with his iron tongs and leather shoulder protector. He was always in a hurry, driven by his perishable product. Unlike the others, he drove an open truck with twenty-five- and fifty-pound cakes of ice stacked in the back, protected from the summer sun only by a heavy tarpaulin. He dripped through the neighborhood as fast as he could, but it was never fast enough! We kids would dart from ambush and jump on the accessible metal step across the rear of the truck. It was great to steal slivers of broken ice. Summer icicles! He always seemed to be looking the other way. Apparently he had been a kid once. And since the sun was going to dispatch the icicles anyway, it didn't matter.

Cardboard signs were stuck in windows indicating the amount of ice desired at each house. Around the corner of Eleanor Avenue, in a vacant lot, was a tiny wooden icehouse. It was fascinating to go inside (it was smaller than a garage) and see the gleaming cakes of ice stacked up in the sawdust, surviving. The cool dark smell and the feel of it, in the dead heat of summer, had an otherworldly quality to it. That little brown house hovers at the very edge of those memories which I can no longer reach.

Fathers would pull their cars up in front of the little house, and the iceman would heave a block of ice onto his leather-covered shoulder

Earliest ice wagon

and then drop it with a reassuring thunk on the back bumper. The point was to hurry home with minimum melt. When I was about seven, our old wooden icebox was replaced with a shiny electric refrigerator, and so was the iceman who never cometh again. Oddly, the word icebox clings tenaciously to our vocabularies.

A vanilla man, as we called him, dressed entirely in black, with a wide, flat black hat and black rain cape, rode on a black bicycle, with a black box strapped on the back fender. He should have been called licorice man, I think. He made his rounds at infrequent intervals, selling vanilla and spices and other Watkins' products.

The white-uniformed milkman in his horse-drawn wagon *clip-clopped* through the motionless dawn and clanked us awake each day with glass milk bottles. When I run out of milk these days (which I do constantly), I think back fondly to the ease of reaching in the wall (milk box door) and finding a day's supply of milk.

People today find it hard to believe that the mailman arrived, wearing indestructible blue, not only at ten o'clock but also at two o'clock day in and day out. Everybody loves a mailman. We loved him twice a day. He even came to our house one Sunday for me to draw his picture.

At noon each day the congenial breadman, in a short-jacketed khaki uniform, sang "Sherlock!" on the front porch, just in time to sweeten lunch. I loved him twice as much as the mailman because he carried a large wicker basket filled with nutrient-free white bread and addicting cream-filled straights and eclairs and orange cookies as big as pancakes. My lifelong addiction to sweets, and eclairs in particular, was born in that damn basket.

The patient horses waited at the curb, stomping and snorting and wetting and so forth. Occasionally we were startled out of our pants by a sudden, furious cascade of liquid hitting the pavement. The volume was inconceivable to us giggling innocents.

The wonderfully arrayed, patient horses.

We kids looked forward to the varied arrivals, and on pleasant days we rushed to each wagon at the curb, daring to step onto the low step and into the driver's tiny wooden work world, daring to touch the leather reins which lay waiting for his return.

We circled the sweet-natured horses, always intrigued by these entries from the animal world into our unextraordinary lives. We tentatively touched their soft noses, stretching up to pat their smooth haunches. They were the only horses I was ever to know, but I can still feel their warm velvet faces and see the blunt little hairs around their nostrils. They were good teachers, providing lasting lessons in patience and constancy.

The men and the horses enlivened our neighborhood and held down their jobs all the days of their lives and all the years of my childhood. We expected them, watched for them in the slow-moving days, and came to know each one as they stitched our lives together with continuity.

The era started ending for the delivery men one spring when Mother reluctantly told the sober little Babcock Dairy man that we were going to have to start buying our milk at the store. He fussed and pleaded and brought us a bowl of whipped cream and all but stamped his foot. It was the most animation we had ever seen him show. But maybe we weren't the first to quit, and he was scared. I don't suppose though that he knew he was taking his first steps toward obsolescence. It was a long time in coming, but it was beginning that morning. No one had any idea.

They were the only horses I was ever to know, but I can still feel their warm velvet faces.

The fathers all went to work at eight o'clock and returned at five, alternating their blue and their gray suits each day. Some took the Eleanor bus which stopped at the corner a few doors away, but most drove the family car, leaving the wives to get groceries and run errands all day Saturday. A few more expensive grocery stores delivered, but lively Nellie Lennex was the only one on our street who ever had any groceries delivered. The Lennexes seemed to have more glamorous food than we did, things like shrimp in aspic and chocolate chip waffles!—not to mention extravagant whipped cream. Across the driveway at our house, Martha and I eagerly attempted to make whipped cream Depression-style by skimming cream off the top of the milk with a little metal contraption (in those days milk was not homogenized, and the cream floated to the top). It wasn't easy, and half the time it didn't whip.

When I was about five, Mother had a minor car accident, caused by her slamming on the accelerator instead of the brake. So she stopped driving. *Forever.* Can you believe it? Anyhow, when she and Daddy went together to get the groceries on Saturdays, it was an event. Daddy was always eager to save a penny, and it seemed they drove all over to get what they wanted rather than purchasing everything at one store. But this was fine with me because it led them to drive to Schauss' Bakery clear down on Monroe Street near the old Avalon Theater! And as I write, I realize, like my mother's search for the perfect sugar cookie, I am still trying to find that wonderful, that golden, that crunchy, that crusty, that nutmeggy, perfect Schauss' fried cake which Daddy brought home by the reckless bagful every Saturday.

During the week, Martha and I were often sent to a small neighborhood Kroger store two blocks away to pick up needed items. It wasn't a country store but it predated supermarkets by a long shot. What made this errand worth the effort was that while responsible little Martha was negotiating Mother's list with the clerk, I was up to my elbow in the Oreo cookie bin. Oreo cookies were perfect then, *and they're perfect now.*

for me — oreo with lid off

← one with double icing for you!

— oreo with bite out. (drawn from model)

Most of the mothers washed on Monday and ironed on Tuesday and stayed at home, working endlessly in pre-appliance industry, never wondering, never questioning, that they might one day be left without a husband, without a pension, without a cent with which to carry on. Some were left wthout any of the above, and it was to be yet another fifty years before women started to wake up and smell something other than coffee.

Mother didn't follow the Monday washday routine, despite her dedication to order. She still moved when the spirit moved her, which was frequently. It didn't matter what day it was. If I happened to see my friend Lois Keller's mother on a Monday, which I often did, she would ask, "Did your mother wash today?" and I would feel guilty answering no. But I think I knew even then that I wasn't going to wash on Monday either.

I'm sure Mrs. Keller also questioned our spotty church attendance, which was in such contrast to the habits of the neighborhood Lutherans. But Daddy said you didn't have to attend church to be decent and honorable, and that's the way I grew up, thinking my father knew it all. And in some ways he did.

One spring afternoon I was walking home from school with my good friend Julia Marie Sullivan. We were splashing our way home through new puddles, chatting away as we so often did. She lived around the corner from me on Eleanor, and we spent a lot of time together. Partly because she was an only child, I was always a welcome guest in her home and at her summer cottage. We were dreamily discussing a movie we had just seen in which Dick Powell had reached out and nearly ignited our dormant puberty. Oh, wasn't he darling (sigh) and wasn't he something when he sang "By A Waterfall" to Ruby Keeler? Oh, swoon. Then I mentioned that Daddy had said that Dick Powell didn't have much of a voice. Julia stopped dead in her tracks. "What makes you think your father knows everything?" she asked.

Needless to say, the thought had never occurred to me. I felt a little hurt and a lot surprised. But I *heard* what she said, and I filed it away for future reference. Was that the very first inkling . . . the absolute very first moment that the separation process began?

Walking back and forth to school each day, through the changing seasons, was a great, freewheeling, shove-'em-into-the-barberry-bushes kind of time. We made friends and memories by the carload on those young, carefree, long daily walks. We kids knew every tree and bush along the streets, every dip and valley on that eight-block trek. We knew every shortcut and where the castor-oil bush was (yuk!). We knew where the principal lived (on our street!). We knew the best climbing trees, and where the ankle-twisting holes were in the vacant lots.

In our neighborhood, we knew to avoid Tarbox's house on Halloween. And we knew we could play under Lennex's back porch, and there would be no spiders. It was as clean as their kitchen.

We knew our neighborhood and the people in it in a way that only children can, with an eye for detail that adults no longer see and with an unerring antenna about people.

The neighborhood trees were young, like the children, barely casting shadows. The houses were all similar, yet different from one another. All new, all built around 1925. Front porches came in all different sizes and provided us with damp and cozy hangouts on rainy days.

Later on in that decade of the thirties, as the grip of the Depression started to ease, some of the neighbors began to have those porches screened in. It was the thing to do. After supper, we would step smartly out onto our new front porch and scan the neighborhood for action. Daddy would check and see the Lennexes on their new porch. "You're not so much!" he'd call to them. Friendly banter drifted back and forth between the houses as the busy sounds of day settled down. At regular intervals, we could hear a distant and reliable *thud-thunk* of cars crossing over the wooden bridge near the Overland plant about a mile away. When I think of summer nights, I can hear that *thud-thunk,* and I can hear the long-ago laughter.

At the mercy of mosquitos for so many years, we were finally liberated, able to escape onto our hard-won porches. Dishes done, games played, the day ending, the neighbors sat proudly in the gathering darkness, rocking and swinging in the newly-available evening air, watching the night sky sparkle with stars and fireflies.

It was a lovely feeling, nestled safely close to our houses, cool and free at last, in that kind of caring atmosphere where you didn't have to try.

Those were the days, my friend.

Chapter 7

*Time is annihilated by intimate
details like these.*

—Unknown

Those days are now all locked into the individual memories of the since scattered gang of kids who shared the 1930s on Overland Parkway in Toledo, Ohio, so typically middle-class, growing tall and wise together on a street named after a car. The factory for the Willys and the Overland and the Whippet (and later the Jeep) was about a mile away, and its seven o'clock factory whistle roused us too early each winter morning in the frosty darkness.

Wait. Come with me. Let's go back to a winter evening in the thirties. Let's do a little window-peeking through time.

It is now twilight. The houses on my block are cozy and reassuringly close together, separated by cement ribbon driveways which lead back to single-car garages. A Hudson, a Ford, a Kissel, a Packard, a Dodge, or a Chevy fill the garages.

It is early in December. The tight little fenced-in backyards are softened and hidden by the snow. The mysterious white mound in the backyard of the house next to ours recalls the overstated rock garden and fish pond which the Lennexes built. With its plump goldfish and its miniature waterfall, it was the neighborhood attraction for a few brief summers.

As darkness deepens, patches of yellow lamplight stretch out on the snow beside our house. A nearly full moon transforms the ordinary little neighborhood into something dreamlike and lovely. Moving carefully among the snowy evergreens, I tiptoe to look in the living room windows on the front of our house. I see us just as we were.

My father is stretched out on the down-filled, rust-colored davenport. His still-dark hair is parted in the middle and combed straight back in the fashion of the day, above a smooth, broad forehead. His blue eyes behind rimless glasses are scanning the newspaper. They are the eyes of someone who observes closely. (One of the things he said most often to me during the long and sometimes deadly Sunday afternoon rides in the family car was "Gin! Sit up and *observe!*" He is a short, muscular man with a congenial face holding leftover sun from summer. He is a man quick to laugh and make others laugh. He is quick to flare up and quick to recover, a man of good will and good sense.

Mother's dark, marcelled hair pulled back in a knot.

Martha took the wind and the rain very seriously.

I see my mother in the dining room, her dark, marcelled hair pulled back in a knot. She is sitting just beyond the wine-colored velvet portiers (as they were called in those days) that separated the living room and dining room. We often closed the portiers because of mysterious "drafts," or used them to hide behind. Mother creates a small silhouette. She is sitting on a footstool in front of a dining room chair on which her sewing machine is placed. The room is dark, except for the small circle of light from the machine's tiny bulb, which is reflected onto her face. A shadow hides in the dimple in her chin. She is secretly making doll clothes for Christmas. She was always secretly making doll clothes. These were little works of art, miniature versions of the little dresses she made her daughters. She does not know it, but she is at her happiest.

My sister Martha is reading in a chair. She is always reading in a chair, her slim, shapely little-girl legs sticking out straight before her, her dark Dutch-boy hair falling forward, hiding her plump cheeks. She is seven or so. She is a serious little girl, responsible and pleasant. She is the classic firstborn child, conscientious, competent, and bright.

Peggy and me, on the right, both eight years old

Early snapshots of Martha reveal a relentlessly solemn little child, very unlike her future self. Mother said she had lots of bewildering fears. Martha took the rain and the wind very seriously. The doctor diagnosed her behavior as a possible reaction to a milk allergy.

I am on the floor playing with our funny dog, Peggy. I am always on the floor playing with our funny dog, Peggy. I am about five. I am not a serious little girl. Nor am I responsible in the way of my older sister. But I am pleasant and make my parents laugh.

The scene changes as I watch. The snow melts, and the doors open. Martha and I spring out of the front door of our house with a detonated velocity born of too much winter. We are out with the rest of the kids to capture the dwindling daylight and the flag. Remember?

The neighborhood is suddenly awash in children, dogs, and spring-blooming things. The kids are named Pinkie and Lois and Joan and Don and two Billys and Bud and Dickie and Patsy and Bucky and Jimmie and Bobby and Marcie. Others from off the block are Julia and Dorothy Mae and Evelyn and Nancy and Mickey and David and Donald and Charles and Phillip and Dynamite Mather.

Martha's "sprinkler queen" trick; neighbor Bud is playing court, while I giggle in appreciation.

The dogs are named Mite (wirehair) and Teddy McGrew (spaniel) and Frank (hunting dog) and Mee Loo (Pekingese) and Spoogit (bulldog) and Wags (wirehair) and Peggy (part bull, part Airedale, part Shetland pony, Daddy always said). Mite died of distemper; Frank moved to Perrysburg; Mee Loo became paralyzed and was put to sleep; Wags was transferred to Arizona; Spoogit was poisoned, accidentally, we presumed. No one knew for sure. (Mrs. Donoher, who lived across from Spoogit Martin, took a little Pyrex dish of what she called "holy water" to sprinkle on the little bulldog who was lying stiffly under a privet hedge in his backyard; the neighborhood kids filed by in morbid fascination as if at a funeral.) Peggy was put to sleep at sixteen (my first brush with sorrow), and Daddy ran over the ancient Teddy, who was sleeping under our car in the shade of a summer noontime.

Peggy's successor, Pudgy, one half chow, one half dalmatian

One more thing about Teddy McGrew. His owner was summoned and, as she and Daddy knelt tearfully behind our Hudson in the driveway, she said kindly, "I'm glad it was you, Mark." She forgave him on the spot because she knew him and also knew he loved dogs, including Teddy the tail-chaser. I stood in the shade nearby, quietly watching, and felt the warm regard she extended to my father.

Don McGrew and Bill Snyder were the two creative boys on the block. They reached their pubescent, chauvinistic zenith, one summer afternoon in 1936 or 1937, with their all-male production of "Cleopotato," given in the Lennex's two-car garage.

Pinkie (Richard) Lennex (supposedly named for Lydia Pinkham's elixir, which his mother Nellie took during his gestation) was a typically pale and scrawny ten-year-old male, and therefore a casting coup as the svelte beauty of the Nile—Cleopotato.

He fell far short of charming in Nellie's red satin formal and black patent-leather high heels as he skidded and fell about in the grease on the garage floor. But still he won our hearts for one summer afternoon as the Egyptian siren. As I recall, the plot was interrupted frequently by long spells of elaborately helpless laughter. By the cast, not the audience.

(from left to right) Peggy, me, neighbor Don McGrew, and Martha in a flowered hat from a school play; about 1928.

The words that Don and Bill had written for their theme song in Cleopotato to the then popular tune, "The Lady in Red," still occasionally float to the surface of my memory and I find myself singing:

> *But the lady is dead*
> *She's pushing up daisies*
> *In her coffin instead.*

Let me add this about Bill:

After lavish messing around on summer mornings, we kids would lounge on the porch-of-the-week. The Lennexes almost always won that award because Mrs. Lennex worked.

Bill and I were twin gigglers, gasping and choking over obscure jokes and situations which no one else seemed to fathom. As his face got redder and redder, his eyes got bluer and bluer. If this took place on a rainy day, I'd be sunk because dampness and exorbitant laughter ("pulmonary gymnastics," my doctor said) would give me asthma.

The two-car garage they used for "Cleopotato" housed a big, boxy, black Kissel and a smaller black Chevy. The Lennex family was the only one on the block with two cars, but the poor economy soon ended that.

The generous area of cement (it seemed Olympic to us kids) in front of that garage provided a wonderful and somewhat daring space for the rollerskaters of the neighborhood to show off their skills. We would come hurtling up the gradual rise of the driveway, veer to the right of the rear corner of the house, and either execute a sweeping arc or crash into the garage doors, hoping someone would or wouldn't see, depending on the degree of success.

Every kid had rollerskates. It was the universal means of propulsion, along with a bike, and a cheap and popular outdoor pastime. It was my very favorite thing to do when spring came. Small armies, all girls, would take off on their skates for nowhere. With skate keys dangling on kitchen strings around our necks, and nothing in our pockets, we would skate for hours. We would trip and fall. Our skates would come loose from our shoes and send us hurtling. Our knees would sing. But on we skated. Our cold cheeks flushed scarlet in the chilly April air. Scenery fuzzed by. Whole springtime whizzed past. Also boys' houses.

We had such a sense of purpose, our tireless legs propelling us into a future we hardly knew was there. We needed no money. We had everything—rollerskates, a skate key, energy, and time.

At night in my bedroom, after a full day on the skates, I'd lie in bed, knees smarting and body tingling, while my aching legs continued to glide down phantom boulevards on phantom skates.

There weren't any "latch key kids" in those days, but once in awhile mother wouldn't get home from a downtown-on-the-bus-all-day-shopping-trip, so she'd leave a key for us on a ledge inside our little "milk bottle door." I usually ignored the key, hoisted myself up and in through the opening, dropping down onto the basement steps. It's hard now to imagine my body then. I suppose I finally got stuck and had to give it up.

Back now to the spring street scene on Overland Parkway that I started to tell you about. All the kids have just dashed down the street to the circle, or posey ring as some called it. It was actually the landscaped hub of a wheel from which six streets branched out, including ours. There it was, a large circle of grass about thirty-five feet in diameter, with high bushes everywhere creating great hiding places. It made an ideal place for a gang to hang out and for kids' games to be played—capture the flag, hide-and-seek, red-light-green-light, pom-pom-pull-away, mother-may-I, kick-the-can, truth-or-consequences, and here-we-come-where-from-Pennsylvania-what's-your-trade-lemonade-show-us-some, and others that have slipped permanently into my subconscious.

Jimmy and Lois Keller

The children are now breathlessly dashing from bush to blooming bush, in and out of the scraps of streetlight and shadow, calling to one another, exuberant and full of the season and themselves. The games are enhanced by a lot of aimless running and screaming, poking and tripping and scaring one another.

The newly-soft air is making it difficult to relinquish the day, but twilight is sifting down now over the cuddled houses and the scattered children. A sharp familiar whistle sends an obedient twosome, Martha and me, flying home. An innocent April day in 1929 has come to a close, holding future shocks at bay. Historical forces shaping our society are closing in.

Black Thursday lies six months in the future.

We watched a dozen springs and autumns come and go in that old posey ring. Finally one windy autumn noontime, as I scuffed through leaves, heading home from school for lunch, I came upon a group of men in *our* circle. They had stuck a sign in the ground that read "WPA." The men were cutting down *our* bushes. I remember

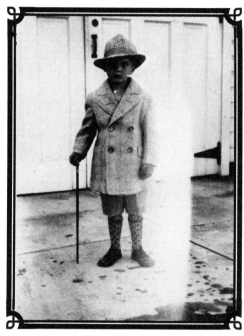

Sportin' Life Pinkie Lennox

feeling disturbed, but I was just old enough, perhaps eleven, to accept it. Our "kids-only" sanctuary vanished that day. It never returned and neither did we, for we were growing up and away.

Chapter 8

We are all balanced on the ledge above the dark.

—Howard Nemerov

By the time I was six years old, the Depression was completely out of control.

I remember the hush that overtook Martha and me when we were told by Mother in October, 1932, that Daddy had been secretly advised to take all his money out of the Ohio Bank. "All his money" undoubtedly didn't amount to much, but still it was an important moment. It seems odd to me now that we, as children, were entrusted with such information. We obviously sensed the moment, because I never told anyone until a few years ago.

On the lunch hour that Mother told us, we were warned that a good family friend would lose his job if we spoke one word. That friend rescued our family's small savings, and I'm told it was not an uncommon occurrence. We weren't the only ones to be saved by a banker friend who reached out at his own terrible risk. How does one repay that debt?

The frightening bank closings changed people's feelings about financial security probably for all time. Businesses went bankrupt. Factories closed. People lost their jobs and were overnight rendered helpless, with no unemployment insurance and no Social Security. Those who were lucky enough, like Daddy, to hold onto their jobs took successive pay cuts.

On another lunch hour, Mother warned Martha and me to behave and not be quarrelsome. Daddy was upset, she said, over a "cut in his salary." I remember searching his face as he sat, rather pensively, over his lunch, to see if he looked any different. . . . I was then only vaguely aware of what exactly a "cut in his salary" meant.

The dread of a job loss was only slightly ameliorated by the fact that others were losing their jobs too. It therefore wasn't as ego-shattering as in more prosperous times, but more than jobs were lost. The people and the country were losing the vision they had of themselves.

The Depression was much more depressing for many beyond the world of Overland Parkway. Even though Toledo was one of the cities in exceptional trouble (with unemployment around 25 percent), our little block in West Toledo knew little of the impoverished straits of people in other parts of the city and the country.

We were lucky and we were young.

There were lots of desperados in those desperate days. The newspapers were full of barbaric tales about John Dillinger, Bonnie and Clyde, Pretty Boy Floyd, and other wild and reckless bank robbers. They were so reckless, they were all gunned down. But Prohibition had created a climate for really big-time crime, a whole new sinister class of bootleggers, racketeers, and hit men. Gang slayings were common and lawlessness was rampant, but it seemed far away.

Yet, just five doors away from our house, facing onto that pastoral posey ring, was a 1920s-style stucco bungalow with a telltale burglar alarm just visible under the eaves. We gave that brooding, shrubbery-enclosed, mute little house a wide berth, because living in it for awhile, right in the midst of our middle-class propriety (accidentally on purpose, no doubt) was a member of the infamous Licavoli gang. We were glad we never saw him or any of his cohorts ever come or go.

By 1933 the Depression had caused twenty-five million people to lose their jobs. Everyone was frightened, for himself and for his neighbor. There were no established federal programs to cushion the blows, as there are today.

And no one knew that a whole generation was going to be scarred.

And no one knew in November of that year (1929), when everyone began wistfully singing a new tune called "Happy Days Are Here Again!" that they were all just "whistlin' Dixie." Happy days weren't gonna be there again until all the singers were a changed people.

As always happens in a disaster, people drew together, sought shelter in a doorway, and sang in the darkness. Families and friends reached out to each other.

Survival was the dominant trait.

President Hoover just didn't get it. He repeatedly proclaimed, "The economy is fundamentally sound." Caught and frozen in conservative old ways of responding to new circumstances, he just didn't get it. He lost the confidence of the people, and he never got it back. He blew it.

As small children, though, and I mean the kids of my small Overland Parkway world, we were only vaguely aware of the muted life-style of the adults around us. I'm sure they never stopped being aware. Fear of losing their jobs dogged our fathers' footsteps.

But we embraced childhood the way kids always have, living from moment to moment while our parents maintained a delicate balance between their fear and our innocence.

Songs of the day showed, as they always do, the mood of the times: "Brother, Can You Spare a Dime?" and "Who's Afraid of the Big Bad Wolf?" Movies provided an escape with slapstick comedians like The Marx Brothers and Charlie Chaplin and Laurel & Hardy. And they lifted spirits with endearing children like Shirley Temple and Freddy Bartholomew. How I loved *those* two!

We didn't eat out often, but when we did, we ate at Bud & Luke's.

Bud & Luke's Restaurant was born in the Depression because we needed it to be born. It helped everyone through those hard times, with cheap and delicious meatloaf and mashed potatoes and vaudevillian-type pranksters for waiters.

As the waiters skidded about, delivering the meals at breakneck speed, they would dust off a bald head with a feather duster, pretend to spill "piping-hot" cardboard coffee into an alarmed lap, slip silverware into a departing guest's pocket and then loudly catch him "in the act." We ate it up, literally and figuratively.

We did jigsaw puzzles until we were cross-eyed; we went to lots of ten-cent movies and listened to a zillion radio shows and made too much fudge and toasted marshmallows over the gas burner on the stove and sang songs from songsheets and went to Toledo Beach and Sand Beach on cheap gas and drove all over hell's half-acre on picnics and camped out on lakes in the nearby Irish Hills of Michigan, and for two weeks every summer we pretended there was no Depression as we vacationed in a house that was fortunately loaned to us in the glorious lake and pine country of northern Michigan.

We did everything that was fun if it didn't cost much.

Chain letters were big. They represented possibility. Bank Night at theaters gave us the illusion that we might get something, might get lucky and win a set of cheap dishes, or collect fifty hankies in a series of chain letters. Since we couldn't have the big things, we went for the small things, like a ten-cent movie with a chance for a win at Bank Night. During the intermission on Wednesday nights (Bank Night), between the double features, the theater manager would step smartly out onto the stage and squint into the darkened, jam-packed theater. He was usually accompanied by a couple of self-important, stage-struck ushers, in mock military uniforms, who stood at attention on each side of the rotating drum which contained the fateful ticket stubs.

Breakfast in a Michigan dawn, 1933

A roadside picnic, on the way to Elk Rapids, Michigan

A hush of greed would fall over the audience as the manager chose someone to come up on the brightly lit stage to draw the lucky ticket number from the drum.

This was serious stuff. It was a homely activity which had one foot in Hicksville and one in Las Vegas.

I remember the story of the daughter of a friend of my grandmother's. Neither the daughter nor her husband had a job. They were down to rock bottom after months of struggling, and she was in a serious depression. One hopeless Wednesday, she was walking along Superior Street downtown, feeling at the end of her rope. She reached over to pick up an envelope she saw on the sidewalk. In it was two dollars. Discouraged and unimpressed by what two dollars could do to change her life, she turned in her tracks and went into the Rivoli Theater to just forget her troubles for a while. You guessed it. She won one thousand dollars at Bank Night. Let me tell you, this was a legendary episode in those hopeless days. So now and then it was more than just a set of cheap dishes.

In 1931 everyone had a major crush on Will Rogers. He was a popular humorist who seemed to reach out and put his arm around the nation. When he made his famous remark, "I never met a man I didn't like," people knew they'd found a friend.

"Everytime Congress makes a law, it's a joke. And every time they make a joke, it's a law," he said. He was a real fun guy.

"Extra! Extra! Read all about it!" the young boys cried. "Will Rogers killed in plane crash!" That was 1935. We literally lost our sense of humor for a while. He left us sobered and alone.

I remember two little children, a shy boy and girl, about five and seven, selling potholders at our front door one raw autumn evening while their uncomfortable mother lingered in the shadows which surrounded our porch. Though I was very young, I felt their embarrassment.

The dignified wife of a talented artist friend of Daddy's sold home-baked bread door to door. And an old, bent-over Jewish man, standing in my memory like a character from "Fiddler on the Roof," came to our door for many summers. He wanted to buy old gold or old clothes. Nobody had either one, at least we never did. The old man had such a bulky look about him. Even on the most blistering July day he seemed to be dressed in layers of dark clothing. A hat, an overcoat, the works. So somebody was selling something to a dangerously overheated old man.

One rainy morning in the late spring of 1931, I opened the screen door to a man who handed me a little card. I was old enough to read that he was deaf and would be grateful for anything we might give him. Mother was always sympathetic, and I watched her feed and give away things to many who came to our door. But for some reason she turned this man away, possibly because there had been too many that week. I went up in the stairway and cried to myself, out of her sight. When she left the door, I quickly grabbed a suede jacket of Daddy's out of the closet at the foot of the stairs and took off down the street after my first "cause." He accepted the jacket with a broad, unused smile. Perhaps he thought Mother had changed her mind. Perhaps he didn't care. I don't remember exactly, but I think Mother was upset.

When I asked my mother's sister, Iona, about her experience during the "Crash," she said in her no-nonsense way, "Well . . . we were all up a creek." She told of the Saturday when she and her real-estate-broker husband went to Lakeside, Ohio, for a vacation. Her husband stopped on the way to deposit in the bank two hundred dollars from a rental that had just been paid him. He owned three cottages on Lake Erie and various other properties (he named Hannaford Drive in Toledo after my father).

On Sunday, Iona sent ten-year-old Roy down to the milk depot to bring back the Sunday paper. Roy returned with the paper and the comment, "Boy, I've never seen so many people at the milk depot!" The shocking headlines announced the closing of the banks. With that closing, of course, came the loss of all their money, including yesterday's two hundred dollars. "How much money have you got?" Albert asked. Together, they had seven dollars and a worthless checkbook. They returned home. They lost their three cottages and other property to bank foreclosures.

That's just one story.

A universal bleakness drifted down like fallout over the entire country. There was nothing to stop our free-fall.

Chapter 9

There is nothing so weak or so powerful as a baby.

—V. H. E.

No one can really reflect on or write about the thirties without considering the impact that the birth of the Dionne quintuplets had on the world. They were one of the brightest spots during the Depression. It's interesting that the things that lifted us the highest were children. They remind everyone that there was sweetness and innocence in life, and that it often belonged uniquely to children.

We had snared the world's treasure in our arms for a little while.

On May 28, 1934, the little Dionne quintuplets were born in northern Ontario. In a time when diversions were limited, the world was caught in a craze of adulation. I adored the doll-like babies. They became the sensation of the nation. I was ten years old, and along with millions of others, "I fell so hard I skinned my knees." I became a collector of the mementos of the little girls that overflowed the market (most of which went out our attic window to oblivion in 1950).

The five identical beauties, born to a simple farm couple, fed the heart-hungry world. The fact that they were not to stay beauties, that they were to suffer incredibly from the accident of their rare birth did not detract from their historic wonder. We were all in love.

The *News-Bee*, an appealing Toledo newspaper for thirty years, ran a daily series of pictures of the little charmers. Every new curl and tooth was catalogued each day for a delighted public. I could hardly wait for the paper to arrive each afternoon with the dear little, doomed little faces peeping up at me from the pink front page.

I cut out all their pictures and made the first of many scrapbooks I was to make during my growing years. (I never have stopped pasting pictures in albums.)

The *News-Bee* ran a coloring contest of the little toddlers, which I won. My picture ran in the paper on Memorial Day of 1936. The paper portrayed me as the ultimate tomboy and, yet, chose to photograph me surrounded by baby dolls. Perhaps the paper captured something accidentally, my struggle to not grow up.

Athletic Artist Who Can Pitch Fast Baseball Wins Cut-Out Prize

—Staff Photo by Clarence Bailey.
Virginia Hannaford displays her prize-winning scrap book of the Dionne babies.

I never have stopped pasting pictures in albums.

It was incredible the way the quint drama literally saved that extremely depressed province of northern Ontario. It became known as "Quintland" and "Little Broadway," and the children became a five hundred million dollar asset, even affecting the price of milk and other products through their endorsements.

The fascination with which the public reacted to these babies had a lot to do with the times. They eased the troubled, worried psyches of a frightened world. It wasn't just Canada and the United States that were so taken with them. They were a true world phenomenon. There were no quintuplets before or none since that were identical and survived.

Included in the glutted market of Dionne memorabilia were five little seven-inch-high dolls with tiny gold heart lockets bearing the name of each child. Mother was able to slowly purchase my three favorites (Annette, Yvonne, and Marie) at $2.98 each. Of course, we were just buying the same doll over and over (lucky Madame Alexander!). There was no individuality to them except for their locket name. By the time Mother could afford the other two, my interests were no longer taken up with dolls. I never completed the set. (The complete set today is valued at a minimum of five hundred dollars.)

There was, of course, no way then that anyone could have known that the dear little backwoods babes would one day live out a tragic scenario written for them by their parents and Dr. DaFoe and the press and the public. The unnatural life they led apart from their parents and siblings, raised by a doctor and round-the-clock nurses in a sterile and isolated environment, yet on display daily to doting crowds, was destined to have damaging effects.

The famous psychiatrist Alfred Adler, wrote recommending the children's return to a normal life with their family (instead of the daily visits "allowed" by Dr. DaFoe). Dr. Adler warned of serious future trouble if the children weren't restored to their family. Because the Canadian government had become the guardian of the girls, Papa Dionne was finally forced to sue to have them returned home.

By then they were ten years old, and it was too late. The damage had been done. They never were able to establish a loving relationship with their parents. They had been irrevocably torn asunder.

It seems somehow tragically appropriate that on the gravestones of Marie and Emilie, each of whom died in her early twenties, are engraved the touching words, "priez pour nous" (pray for us).

Chapter 10

On a very wide front and in the truest possible sense, Franklin D. Roosevelt included the excluded. F.D.R. was a man of intense sympathy.

—Joseph Alsop

Enter Franklin D. Roosevelt and the necessity and the humanity of the New Deal.

Growing up then meant Roosevelt. He, as a president but also as a personality, was woven in and out of our everyday lives. Radio was the perfect medium for his eloquence and warmth. He was the message—encouraging, quotable and hopeful.

On an early autumn evening in 1932, Mother stood in the living room with her back to the mantle, wearing glasses for the first time. I sat on the floor, studying her new, more mature look. She said, "Mark, I'm going to vote for Roosevelt." Daddy, from a staunch Republican family, said, "Well, Eddie, you'll just cancel my vote." Mother was adamant. Her concern for the underdog had caused her to align with Roosevelt's yet unlegislated dreams.

On another evening in that same fortuitous autumn, Martha and I were taken down to the Union Station. Roosevelt was coming to the station on a whistle-stop tour. Daddy held me horizontally up and over the heads of the crowd to enable me to shake Roosevelt's hand (which I did) as he reached out to the crowd from the train's rear platform. As he stood there, no one was really aware, nor were we ever, of the extent to which polio had crippled him. It was a carefully guarded secret then. I knew I was doing something that I'd remember. I was injected at that moment with a political interest that has never left me.

November 1932 came. Little red voting booths (one-room houses on wheels), complete with stoves and chimneys, were rolled out into vacant lots all over town. Long after the early November darkness had fallen over the city, lights burned in the little red houses, and thin lines of smoke rose into the expectant autumn air.

Mother, wearing her new glasses, had marched off smartly that morning to vote in our vacant lot at the corner. Of course, she voted for the man with the gift of empathy. Daddy voted for Hoover. He voted Republican only one more time.

For the balance of Roosevelt's lengthy and controversial reign, we were among his enthusiastic supporters. Even as children, Martha and I felt the excitement generated by his "Fireside Chats" on radio. We were also enthralled by his larger than life presence in newsreels and movie theaters. We went frequently to movies, because Daddy got free passes from the newspaper where he worked. So I became hooked on Roosevelt and liberal causes and the movies a long time ago.

Daddy soon fell under the spell cast by this patrician figure from Harvard and from the Hudson River Valley aristocracy. But what appealed to Daddy was Roosevelt's humor and his common touch. Roosevelt was as close to being a movie star with his "presence" as JFK was to one day be, and he radiated a zest few could ignore in those days when zest was a rare commodity.

It was as if he were pulling a drowning nation to shore, and the nation had a death grip on him. It is difficult to overstate how he buoyed the spirit.

Ya hadda been there.

As a child, I was impressed that Roosevelt was a rich man who cared about poor people. He never became hardened and indifferent to the suffering of those who had not grown up as privileged as he. He was a hero to me and a true champion of the downtrodden. I loved FDR for the same reason that I admired Dickens. Each sought to transform the world in which he lived.

In 1936 I began betting—and winning—on elections. (I won thirty cents that year. Later on, when Harry Truman ran against Dewey, I earned myself a small reputation by sensing that outcome. I still can usually manage to win a pleasant lunch from a friend.) I was suddenly passionate about something besides my own life. With limited knowledge, I was consumed by a new awareness, a "global" view from the second seat, fourth row, gleaned from *The Weekly Reader.*

That same year when FDR won his second term by an unprece-
dented landslide, someone said, "If Landon had given one more
speech, Roosevelt would have won Canada too."

The welfare and social programs that FDR initiated
created an almost pathological hatred in many Americans. These were
usually people who seemed reasonably comfortable, the so-called
"smug minority," who resented paying into a system that was going to
create "a bunch of lazy bums!" In my view, the people who hated
FDR, with an almost frightening intensity, had developed an attitude
of "I've got mine, now you get yours." It seems to me they weren't
taking into account our vastly different abilities. Many poor people are
so busy trying to survive economically, they don't have leftover energy
to motivate and encourage their kids.

In all fairness, people feared that the government would do too
much for people and empty them of their initiative. But when you
have inherited despair, it is often impossible to pull yourself up by your
bootstraps. You can't if you don't have any boots.

John Steinbeck wrote in Esquire Magazine, "Much later, when
business picked up, business leaders howled with rage against government control and Roosevelt. They seemed to forget that they had laid
their heads in his lap and wept, begged him to take over."

The blue eagle symbol of the NRA (National Recovery Act) was
soon everywhere, even on kids' bikes. It was as popular as the yo-yo.
To us, the eagle meant better times were just around the corner.
However, the NRA was declared unconstitutional and was gone by
1935.

Meanwhile, the WPA and the PWA and the CCC and a dozen
other such programs became the lifeboats which carried many unfortu-
nate people to a safe harbor on the other side of the Depression.

And FDR's Social Security program, scorned by so many, yet today
eagerly received by all, was yet another indication of the humanity of
those days of despair.

We were a wise and lucky country to have chosen FDR as our leader
during that time in history. If ever we needed an innovative man, it
was then.

I like to think of myself as an independent because I've often voted
for Republicans. But for the most part, I'm kidding myself. I'm nearly
always drawn back to those combined early influences of the Depression, Roosevelt, and my parents. In my head I'm an independent, and
in my heart I'm a liberal.

No sooner had the stressful years of the Depression eased than we were thrown into the traumatic years of World War II, all of this under the reassuring leadership of Franklin Roosevelt who was elected president by a landslide four times.

In early 1945 Roosevelt and the other allied leaders held their last strategic wartime meeting at Yalta on the Black Sea. In the heady atmosphere of impending victory, few people noticed that President Roosevelt's contagious spirit and indomitable optimism were depleted.

On a suddenly warm April afternoon in 1945, I (then age twenty) was riding in my friend Phyl Catlan's carful of high-spirited Tri-Delta sorority sisters from the University of Toledo. We were on our way out to one of our legendary hangouts, The Frozen Custard.

The car was alive with spring fever and yearning, yearning for the boys who were still war-scattered from England to Burma to Okinawa, and just yearning in general. The music on the car radio was suddenly interrupted with the impossible news of the death of the man who had dominated our national life for twelve long years.

Always emotionally ready to spill over in any direction, I cried. Otherwise, the car was quiet and stunned, each friend feeling the impact in her own way. We quickly returned to the university to listen to the uniquely authoritative radio voice of H. V. Kaltenborn, followed by our unlikely new president, Harry Truman, giving his ineloquent and soon-to-be-famous "load of hay" reaction. What we were all feeling, besides the fear and confusion of the wartime loss, feeling without knowing it, was that a tender and innocent part of our youth had died along with the only president we had ever known.

We were twenty years old and knew that we would never be utterly young again.

Chapter 11

*There was a child went forth
every day,
And the first object he look'd upon,
That object he became,
The early lilacs became part of
the child.*

—Walt Whitman

The light that fell on those early days was a different, younger light, and it shines on my recall like flattering stage lighting, turning our backyard into a late-blooming valentine.

One time Daddy, uncharacteristically, went to a dinner meeting at Pilgrim Congregational Church near where we lived, and where Martha and I attended Sunday school off and on. Mostly off. Daddy was unaware that he was sitting next to the minister, and when he was asked by him, "What church do you attend, Mr. Hannaford?" Daddy replied, "My church is my backyard."

When warm weather eased into the neighborhood, our backyard was unique on the block. It was a playpen, a toy store, a gym, a hangout, a valentine, and a church. It was clearly the backyard of an artist, and of a young man and woman who put their children ahead of most other things. A man that Daddy worked with once said to him, "Lord, Mark, you'd think those children ran your life!"—to which Daddy happily replied, "They do."

Daddy built the most marvelous playthings. He was very inventive, as I've said, and good with his hands. He applied his art in many practical ways. We had a unique sandbox, which stood eighteen inches off the ground, with seats on each side to keep small bottoms out of damp sand. It was topped with a large umbrella and should have been patented, and marketed along with a number of his other inventions, which the Depression stifled.

Behind the garage where our Hudson grew to maturity and beyond was a splendid grape arbor. It sheltered the special sandbox and dappled us and the plump blue grapes with sunlight for six months out of the year. The flickering shadowed repose of the arbor lured the neighbor children there, first to make sand pies and later to plan elaborate golf courses (with little mirrors for lakes).

Our "south forty," 1928

Our two-tiered sandbox, designed to keep small bottoms out of damp sand

In this same innocent arbor, the small son of the doctor who lived across the street pulled down his shorts and showed the little girls something they hadn't seen before.

Looking out of my bedroom windows on moonlit nights, I could see the clumps of smoky blue grapes and could smell them ripening in the moonlight. Lying in bed, I would picture in my mind the familiar outdoor things of daytime with all the daylight removed. I'd imagine the swings stirring easily in the pale shadows, the varied flowers of morning—the reds and purples and yellows and oranges—now iced blue by a distant moon. I see the tall darkened poplars shimmering like aspens, like money trees, the plump goldfish in Lennex's pond next door, sleeping suspended in their wet world, the neighborhood cars, quiet and cooling in their dark garages, all the spinning bikes at rest, and the frisky neighborhood dogs now sleeping cool and still in neighbor basements or content on neighbor beds.

The summer night sounds of crickets would slip into my room, and I would sing in the darkness the songs my parents sang in the daylight, singing myself to sleep.

It must have been a pleasant sound for them. What parental heart wouldn't warm to the sound of untroubled childhood, singing unselfconsciously in the darkness?

We had two rope swings, one high, one low, to accommodate growing legs, and a trapeze where we were daring young women. Early one July evening, I ran hollering out the back door after a scary radio session with Omar, The Wizard of Persia. I flew across the yard, grabbed the trapeze, flipped around in a dazzling twilit performance and fell thud on my back. I had never had the wind knocked out of me before and, as the dust settled around me, I rose in a trance and walked mechanically out of the yard. I was on a death-march, or so I thought.

We also had a little two-seater wooden swing in which two children could sit facing each other. It was a cozy affair where little ones could exchange secrets and share cookies to the intimate croon of its squeak and glide. One or two kids could stand up, urging the swing ever higher and higher, threatening to dump us all. (Sound of shrieking!) It was also a good place to suddenly shove the one standing up out into the grass. (Shriek!) The intimacy was neat, but the shoving was neater.

To complete this catalog of yard equipment, we had a lawnful of canvas chairs and there was even a permanent little table for tea parties under the pussy willow tree.

In conclusion, there was an adult glider, which seated four big people, and a children's canvas and wood rocker which always—I mean, *always*—sharply pinched little fingers. Our parents thought of everything except destroying that malevolent little chair. It survived into our adolescence, pinching somebody's fingers on a regular basis until we grew up and moved away, and the little chair slipped into history.

A cozy affair for the exchange of secrets

There were no swimming pools available to the neighborhood kids in those days, so the big summer deal was running in the sprinkler or sitting in a galvanized tub of water in the yard.

To make it seem more than it was, we'd wait one hour after lunch before going in the water. We'd all heard our mothers call this warning at Toledo Beach and nearby lakes. I remember the pathetic waiting.

I'd sit in my bathing suit while the sprinkler sprinkled tantalizingly nearby. Always part rebel, I could just take so much and, after about half an hour, I would suddenly dash into the sprinkler and begin the litany of sprinkler tricks: 1) stand in middle of, like a statue, 2) put on head, like a queen, 3) sit on and bring to temporary halt, and 4) unscrew sprinkler, squirt everything in sight with hose.

The bathing cap made this tub seem like a swimming pool; Joan Lennex is my buddy.

I wore an orange wool bathing suit with two disgusting butterfly designs on it. I have no idea now what caused my overnight revulsion for that suit. When I was seven, the little orange suit was just fine with me. When I was eight, I hid in a sweltering tent up at Mud(!) Lake, waiting for a chance to dash into the lake without being seen. I could then sit on the bottom, and no one would know my submerged secret. When Mother finally forced me out of the tent and into the open, I ran pell-mell toward the lake, with one hand glued to my left shoulder and the other to my right hip, successfully concealing the horrid design.

All the neighborhood backyards were separated by wood and wire fences. Walking fences, which we did frequently, was an activity which vanished with that style of fencing. In our yard, the fences were climbed upon by lavender sweet peas, and the grass was bordered by iris and tulips and bleeding hearts and daisies and poppies. It was a garden fit for poets.

Daddy knelt with me before the bleeding heart bush one May morning when I was very small and held one of the incredible little grieving hearts in the palm of his strong, square hand. He marveled at the heart's intricate perfection. Now, fifty years later, I go into my own garden each spring and hold the delicate, incredible little heart in the palm of my hand and marvel and remember. And when I go to New York, my son takes me into his garden and shows me his bleeding heart bushes. Maybe one day Elizabeth and Rebecca, his little toddlers, will kneel in some future garden and perpetutate their great-grandfather's love of little hearts.

Everywhere one looked in our yard, there was an artful blend of beauty and utility. Lilacs concealed the telephone pole and the garbage can (we only had *one* in those days) and lilies of the valley hid the coal chute by the driveway. Spirea bushes dripped everywhere, their musky odor mingling with the smell of mint that grew alongside the garage by the swing set. Mint still gives me a vague feeling of nausea because I used to twist and twist in my rope swing, releasing it suddenly in a mad twirl, as nausea and mint pervaded my senses in a permanent blend. A row of slim young poplar trees across the back of the yard grew tall with us, scattered a thousand sunsets, and buffered the west wind. A prolific Paul Scarlet climbing rose arched over the trellis above our garden gate, outside the breakfast nook window. It turned our June morning kitchen into a rose-colored bower and provided last-day-of-school bouquets for teachers. I knew I would always remember the aroma and color of those mornings. The yard I remember, that fragrant and nurturing haven, is still near a doorway in my mind, splashed with color and always on call, a door which is slightly ajar, allowing me more and more frequent entry. Can you picture the intense poppies, the stark tulips, the grieving bleeding hearts, the fragrant roses, the sun-soaked buttercups, the "sweet violets, sweeter than all the roses," and "that child of air lingering in the garden there"?

Summers ago
kneeling in the garden,
mother—young and supple
in a sleeveless housedress—
tenderly cups her hand
around the flaming cup
of an Oriental poppy. . . .
its black smoky center
necessary to its art

Four years old,
kneeling near Mother
in the warm earth,
close to the
flaming silken tissue
with the black heart

I watch Mother
sever the moment
with a trowel
halving a grubworm
at the poppy's base

Beauty and the beast

—VIIE, October 1983

Chapter 12

The chief agony of parenthood is that we can never take the blows intended for another.

—John Mason Brown

Summer, 1935. The time had come for me to investigate Martha's sometimes baffling behavior. She periodically took to her bed with a mysterious malaise. I had seen a little book she made efforts to hide from me called *Marjorie Mae's Twelfth Birthday*. Her efforts, of course, cemented my resolve to find the secret opus. Lois Keller lived across the street and was just my age. After some minor detective work, Lois and I found the tiny booklet hidden under Martha's mattress. Lois didn't have an older sister, she was the oldest of three. Equally uninformed, we read the little book together. We carefully examined each sentence, looking in vain for clues. But the shrouded language of the era left us as baffled about Martha's strange malady as it had before we had read it.

Lois and I came to the conclusion that Martha must be suffering from "enlightenment." That was the big word in the book we weren't familiar with. We knew that we too could be suffering from enlightenment someday soon.

But since our bodies and minds were temporarily out of sync, we put aside our curiosity and let nature take care of it in her own good time.

The endless summer wore on. One memorable morning I was sitting in the big mahogany rocker in the bedroom Martha and I now shared, and I was looking at the latest full-color picture book of the Dionne quintuplets, utterly entranced.

I didn't know it, but that morning I had one foot in the past and one foot in the future. One minute I was a little girl in a big rocker, idolizing five adorable babies; the next moment I was startled by the unexpected arrival of enlightenment, my uninvited and intimate guest for the next forty years. Take it or leave it. I was nearly eleven.

It is my recollection that most young ladies my age took this event in their stride. If anything, they welcomed it in their eagerness to grow up.

My first reaction was alarm. I ran down to the kitchen in tears. Mother and Martha were standing in front of the stove. Martha rolled her eyes at my reaction. Mother was comforting, but I spent the rest of the day feeling displaced and angry.

My fearful tears would have easily revealed, to anyone who understood such things, that I was reacting to the subconscious feelings of insecurity that growing up and growing away would bring.

I didn't understand why I was angry. I'm sure it was based on fear. The only fear I ever remember having as a child was the fear related to periodic bouts of asthma triggered by my relatively frequent colds. I was fearful about who would take care of me when I grew up and had asthma and my parents would be dead.

There was virtually no medication for asthma then. The only ally I had in my struggle to breathe against the terrible constriction in my chest was my mother's tender ministration.

She was always nearby, always listening for the slightest wheeze. But she couldn't breathe for me, much as she wanted to. Many years later I wept for my new little son, as he struggled for breath in my arms and I wanted to breathe for him. And I thought about my mother.

Time and technology meanwhile had intervened, and Richie was to have the help of instant medication.

Back in the thirties, about the only thing Mother could do was swab menthol rub on my chest. It didn't help. I just had to tough it out until morning because it was so difficult to lie down and breathe at the same time. When dawn would finally come, washing the sheets and walls and my toys in welcome blue light, I was ready to get up. I needed to be vertical. Asthma had stretched me and the night to the breaking point.

When my mother's mother was dying from heart failure, following a severe, first-time-ever asthma attack back in 1936, she said to the doctor, "I caught this from my little granddaughter." "Oh, no," he said, "your little granddaughter got it from you." We all knew, of course, that it was inherited, but it seemed odd that Grandmother had never had asthma before.

At the same time my grandmother was dying, I caught a terrible cold and experienced the worst asthma I had ever had. Mother gave me a pill that had been given to Grandmother. It was ephedrine. It was a miracle.

Despite my occasional week-long sieges with asthma, I had always been an energetic tomboy, climbing and sliding and playing baseball and football. I now became even more dedicated to those "manly" pursuits. I pretended to my baffled mother that the aforementioned anger was because I wouldn't be able to play ball anymore. Actually, I was bewildered. I was simply afraid of growing up. Anger was the only tool I had to hold off the inevitable—ineffectual and pointless as it was. I fought like a tiger to hold onto the protective atmosphere in which I had been reared.

Summer 1936. One gray, sultry, boring August afternoon I wandered into Mother's bedroom, dressed only in a pair of cotton underpants. I was twelve and sporting a brand-new bosom. As I recall, I wasn't very impressed by the advent of this development. There was no way I could have known of the feverish preoccupation with the female breast that would eventually overtake the world after Queen Victoria was finally and totally laid to rest. It didn't seem like much of a deal to me, although when friend Julia and I slept overnight at each other's homes, we checked up on one another's progress. She was way ahead of me in the bosom department, but then I surged ahead in the pelvic region. It was nip and tuck for a while, but she eventually won hands down in the bosom category and remains supreme to this day, no doubt. Our innocence was as wide as the sky. We giggled and compared and had no idea.

That boring, sultry day. I sat down on the foot of Mother's bed and was dreamily looking out the front window at the empty neighborhood, alternately checking myself out in Mother's big vanity mirror opposite the foot of her bed. I neglected to check the window to my right.

I thought I heard something. Someone was giggling. A lot. My eyes darted around and came to rest with horror on the lascivious, twelve-year-old face of Pinkie Lennex, peering under the partially raised venetian blind of his bathroom window across the driveway. Since I was sitting topless in full daylight, I knew the beans had been spilled. I dropped to the floor, blushing violently, my heart pounding. My exit was accompanied only by the sound of laughter.

I did not look Pinkie in the face again until after World War II.

Autumn, 1936. One chilly October afternoon, my father stepped off the Eleanor bus after work and witnessed a particularly rough game of football in the corner field, in which his youngest daughter ended up on the bottom of a pile of neighborhood huskies.

I was promptly called home and was informed that I had just played my last game of football in the corner lot. We didn't resist a fully resolute command from Daddy. We knew when he meant business.

After supper, as the football game at the corner resumed, I climbed moodily up on the built-in buffet in the dining room to pout. I looked morosely out the windows over the buffet down the street at the silhouetted figures still playing ball in the approaching autumn dusk. Daddy ignored my misery. I felt desperately sorry for myself.

But nature works wonders. I sulked awhile, curled up in the corner on the buffet. I felt that somehow I was watching my childhood disappear. Of course, that's exactly what I was doing, but pretty soon (say fifteen minutes) my mourning period ended. I jumped down from my perch on the buffet and decided to finally get on with the business of growing up.

The following autumn, on one of those dear old golden-rule days, sitting in our rigid, wooden, nailed-to-the-floor school desks, both Dick Dunham and I reached down to pick up the pencil I had dropped. Our hands accidentally touched. I looked down at the top of his dark curly hair. He glanced up at me, his dark-lashed blue eyes like just discovered art objects. At last I understood. I had been let in on the mystery of Scarlett and Rhett. I had my first crush.

Martha and I were a country mile from being class beauties, but we enjoyed a lot of popularity with both boys and girls. Many years later, my eighth-grade teacher, Sylvia Molter (everybody's favorite), with whom my family became good friends, told me that she had heard about me long before she had me as a student. She said she was curious to find out what it was that made me seem special to lots of kids (because it was certainly not my looks).

I can talk about it now that years have gone by without feeling that I'm boasting, because I understand the why of it.

Mrs. Molter told me that she discovered that I had "such a generous feeling toward other people." I realize now that it was the spirit with which my parents surrounded me that gave me empathy toward others. It was this spirit and my father's sense of humor in particular which enabled me to move easily into and through adolescence. Because my parents accepted me totally, I accepted myself. One day in class Mrs. Molter looked at me and said, "You must have wonderful parents." I didn't know what the heck she meant, then.

She was the kind of teacher every kid likes to have. She inspired us and laughed with us and wore shocking pink knit dresses (other teachers all wore Depression colors) and scolded us with her eyes smiling.

Daddy's most persistent advice, beyond "Sit up and observe," was "Be yourself." He said it over and over again. So, in a period of awful self-consciousness for many, I was reasonably relaxed and content. My self-esteem had been secured years earlier. I had by now made peace with my rapidly advancing maturity and was enjoying the attendant benefits. I seemed to miss out on most of the awkward feelings so many kids experience.

Billy Snyder, Martha (at the wheel), Don Shunk, and David Evans

I am sure now that the boys hung around because, like the rest of the world, they liked and needed to feel at ease. And because I did, they did. They just wanted to be comfortable, especially at that age. I think it's that simple. So my first entry into that often traumatizing social world of puberty was pleasant and flattering for me.

Grade-school age was a truly innocent time. There wasn't any kissing going on behind our garage that made the boys hang out at our house. I'm sure some of the mothers might have thought that Martha and I, not being all that pretty, must be doing *something* to attract the boys. But it was a matter of self-esteem, pure and simple.

One snowy winter dusk, as Martha and I stood at the kitchen sink doing the dishes and singing the popular songs of the day, we suddenly jumped back in surprise.

Two windows over our kitchen sink faced the driveway, about eight feet off the ground. Suddenly, a disembodied head hurtled into view for an instant and then plummeted from sight. Then another and another. First, our kitchen light caught the winter-reddened face of Warren, then Phillip, then Keith. The love-struck adolescent boys, like frogs, were leaping in our snowy driveway, thrusting themselves vertically upwards to try to catch Martha's attention. It was a mating ritual if ever we were to see one. She was thirteen and delighted. I was eleven and didn't get it, yet.

Before long, the boys tired of leaping at the windows. Martha and I continued to stare expectantly. Slowly, a large wooden letter K, formed by one of those long, skinny, folding rulers, rose into view. We waited. The K sank from sight. There was a brief pause. Then the letter W appeared . . . K.W., the initials of the boy Martha had a crush on! The boys outside continued their antics, but with deteriorating creativity as they slowly froze.

As the seasons changed, the gyrations in the winter darkness changed. The boys shifted from awkward adolescence to phony sophistication and back again, as uncertain as their changing voices.

Chapter 13

There is always one moment in childhood when the door opens and lets the future in.

—Graham Greene

Our house was always so tidy. There was none of the tumult of magazines and books and half-finished projects, which were to one day clutter my own home. Mother was orderly, and had artistic leanings, so she created a pleasant and welcoming home.

As a true nature lover, Daddy did his best to make his small plot of land into a nature preserve with swings. It was memorable.

All of this would have remained terrific if I hadn't seen Paree or, in this case, a house in Perrysburg one electrifying autumn weekend.

With a brush in his hand, Daddy became a man possessed. When he wasn't creating commercial art or doing portraits, he was prowling, brush at the ready; his eyes scanning furniture, walls, yard stuff; seeking any surface to paint, mostly green.

I slept in a green bed; put my shoes and socks on while sitting in a green chair; ate in a green kitchen; and grew up, in spite of it, loving the color green.

In my room, on the green (sigh) ivy wallpaper, above the green bed, hung a green-framed picture with lots of little elves sitting along a tree branch. Daddy was fascinated with imps and elves and spent most of his spare time at his drawing board creating large nature paintings to serve as backdrops for his imps.

He created many original games and toys and colorbooks, and he never seemed to deplete his creativity. He met with only limited success in getting his ideas marketed. In an economy where money was seldom spent on unnecessary things, he dealt with a lot of disappointments and heartaches that we kids never knew about.

The flowers and imps Daddy loved to paint;
he would have made a great artist for the Disney studios.

Meanwhile, out in California, another young artist was drawing mice and imps in nature settings. He was Walt Disney, and in 1937 his full-length cartoon *Snow White* hit the nation like an adolescent crush. That same year Daddy was offered a job at the Disney Studios on a six-month trial basis. If he proved himself, he would be hired.

Still fearful in those days, Daddy turned down his one big chance.

A self-portrait; Daddy used the shutter timer on his much traveled camera.

Daddy loved to share his pictures with all children, not just his own kids.

In that thirties' atmosphere, Disney and Daddy came along at the perfect time. You could even say that they had a date with destiny, and that Daddy didn't show up.

Compounding his own uncertainties, Martha and I were getting older and fussed about leaving our friends. For whatever part we played in his decision (and I suspect it was large), I have been haunted by the thought that we kept him from going west.

I suspect this lost opportunity might have been the high-water mark of the life of a man brimming with talent. I now see that after that his creative energy seemed to stall. He had made the decision that cost him certain recognition and probable wealth. He enjoyed reasonable success, but he never reached the heights his promise indicated.

Memories seem to get caught in kitchen corners. I think that when most people reflect on their early lives, they timewarp back into their childhood kitchens, kitchens full of sunlight and the sweet aroma of cinnamon rolls and the warm feelings conjured up when life is *okay*.

Our kitchen was sunlight yellow and Daddy green. Green trim was on everything trimmable. Through the kitchen windows, over the sink and past the green windowsills, we made faces at Joan and Pinkie Lennex in their kitchen. And we waved at each other over a thousand, thousand dishwashings. It was through these windows that Mother caught repeated glimpses of "Little Joan" as she took on more and more homemaking responsibilities following her father's death and her mother's need to hold down a job. Mother tried to inspire me to be more of a little homemaker, more of a wee cook, like Joan. But her "look at little Joan" ploy flopped.

Something I don't miss at all from the old days was that rite of spring that virtually turned our houses inside out. The elaborate, exhausting spring housecleaning ritual, which moved half the contents of the houses onto the front porches to air out, was just what every family did.

There was a special kind of transformation at the end of the day when the April-fresh furniture returned to new positions in the living room, and Mother put fresh bouquets of lilacs and tulips on each end of the mantle, and the room would be in softly lit, lilac-scented order.

That house was just about all a kid could want. Then, one day when I was eleven years old, I was invited to stay over with Patsy. She was a young neighbor who had moved to Perrysburg with her family and their dog, Frank. Perrysburg is a suburb of Toledo, overlooking the Maumee River.

When Patsy lived across the street from us, I liked to go upstairs in her house and lie on her parents' bed, so I could look up into the mouth and nostrils of a dark, forbidding stuffed moose. It was so low over the bed I could easily reach up and put my fingers in its hairy nostrils. It was the only moose I ever did that to.

It's hard now for me to imagine any kind of romance with an ugly chaperone like that, but at that time I thought beds were just for sleeping.

Patsy's father was a doctor and an unusual man of many interests. One summer morning I walked into their kitchen, and Patsy's year-old baby brother was seated in his high chair screaming wildly. He had tubes descending from each nostril, which ran down to a bottle on the floor connected to a motor. The poor babe was plugged in by the nose. I looked at him in horror while the mother calmly explained that the tubes were suctioning out mucus because he had a cold. Yuk!

Getting into Patsy's new home in Perrysburg was risky business. At the front door sill was a mini-railroad crossing for high-speed Lionel trains. The trains circled the outside walls of the entire downstairs, making pedestrian travel hazardous. I spent the weekend tripping over unexpected tracks that emerged suddenly from under flounces of easy chairs.

Upstairs, two bedrooms had been converted into one long, shooting gallery. There was an opening in the far wall with moving targets, like ducks that slid by at a carnival.

On the next afternoon, Patsy and I went to visit a little friend of hers nearby. I walked into that friend's front door and into a different world.

We entered a huge center hall to the right of which were two spacious, sun-filled, and startling rooms. The first room had a pale, turquoise-blue baby grand piano in one corner. There were peach-colored satin draperies at the windows and pea-green velvet chairs scattered about.

The next room, rather like a sun room, was filled with plump white leather couches against black shiny walls with large mirrors. It was 1936.

I was flabbergasted. We had seen opulence in the movies, along with the evening-gowned or negligéed movie queens, but it was never the real world to us. Now here was movie-land elegance not just on planet Earth, but right here, an automobile ride from home.

Patsy's little friend took us up to her mother's bedroom to look for some money so we could walk to the drug store and buy some ice cream. She began opening bureau drawers. She opened a drawer filled with purses, then another drawer filled with purses, and then another. I was transfixed. There must have been twenty or thirty purses. She rummaged through three or four until she got enough money for ice cream.

I had such an odd feeling. I thought of my mother's two purses, one for summer, one for winter. It was just a momentary flash of a thought, and then we went bounding off to the store. But I was aware for the very first time of what my parents did not have, what they had been doing without. It was my first clash with reality.

On the second afternoon of my visit, I was to be startled again. I was wearing a navy blue knitted dress with a red and white stripe circling my still flat sixth-grader's chest. We were in Patsy's large white tile bathroom. The window was open, and warm October air was moving curtains. I was waiting for Patsy to finish and pull up her panties, when she said, "Do you know how babies are made?" (Here I'll remind you that she was the older sister of the boy who took down his shorts in the grape arbor.) I didn't have the foggiest notion, although my friend Julia's mother had given Julia and me a book to read one night about a year earlier when I had slept over. It was entitled *Growing Up*. We were lounging on her bed, talking the endless talk of ten-year-olds. We browsed halfheartedly through the book as her mother self-consciously retreated into the darkened upstairs hallway. We didn't know what the heck it was all about. A seed from the father? What kind of seed? We exchanged puzzled glances. A seed! How! Where! We didn't get it, and we didn't care that we didn't get it. It was obviously too soon for my buddy Julia and me, although we were nearly eleven.

So Patsy straightened me out in the informed frank language of the daughter of a doctor. She slammed the door on my innocence. It couldn't have lasted much longer anyway.

I returned home on Sunday afternoon, from that weekend in Perrysburg, a somewhat estranged eleven-year-old, certainly not the one who had left two days earlier on the Rossford bus.

To begin with, I was shocked to discover, walking into our living room, that it was not the house I had loved so uncritically for so long. Overnight it had become unfashionable and plain. The rug appeared threadbare. The rooms, so recently beloved, were spartan and suddenly featureless.

I flopped down on the old rust-colored davenport. "The Music Goes Round and Round," the big hit of the day, was playing on the radio. I felt strange, disillusioned, guilty about my feelings. My beliefs had loosened and were wandering.

I was suddenly aware that beyond the world of Overland Parkway there might be any number of worlds, any number of Hollywood sets where life was *real*. My value system was suddenly in disarray. All those sweet and mellow evenings by the radio, eating popcorn and drinking grape juice; summer afternoons gasping and sweltering for the love of it in a backyard tent; lavender twilights with fireflies like low-flying stars, like celebrations; cool rainy days for making fudge and playing on damp porches. All of this suddenly seemed like old stuff, passé, over.

The tomboy I had been was soon to give up baseball and football and marbles and retire permanently to the bench.

All of a sudden it came to me that Mother and Daddy had been up to no good. How else had they produced Martha and me? Yuk!

I was moody, curious, and puzzled. Influences, both inner and outer, were at work. I was moving to new rhythms of which I was only vaguely aware. Mother and Daddy, sensitive and flexible, accommodated most changes. For the most part they did not interrupt my new introspection. They accepted me pretty much as I was at any given moment. This is not to suggest that they didn't get plenty sick of my moods. There were encounters but, in general, they dealt with good humor and acceptance. There was nothing in those adolescent days to compare with the rebellion of teenagers thirty years later.

My parents, along with an accident of genetics, are responsible for my luckiest quality, good mental health. It could so easily have gone the other way, in the light of all the unstable people we had in our family.

My parents were going to miss the funny notes I wrote and put on their bed each night, along with their nightclothes laid out in accidentally provocative positions. They were going to miss those Friday nights with Jim Ameche and Martha and me. They would miss my singing in the darkness. There were plenty of things they wouldn't miss too, but I didn't feel there was anything I'd miss. I was too full of enigmatic new feelings to bother with that kid stuff anymore. I was growing up.

But Mother and Daddy didn't hold on. They loosened the reins just a little and began the process of letting go.

Chapter 14

The way we weave the web of emotion between ourselves and others is patterned on what we had with our mother.

—Nancy Friday

For a few short summers in the late thirties, when Martha and I were about fifteen and thirteen and Mother was still young, we were three young women together. Martha and I had crossed over an imaginary line and had become Mother's "gang" for a while. We were catching up with her. It was a brief interlude.

On summer mornings, often fresh from finishing the laundry together in the cool basement; fresh from the routine of feeding cool, wet clothes through the wringer and hanging the bright summer dresses on the lines that crisscrossed our backyard, the three of us sprawled over the living room furniture like kids at summer camp. Mother didn't sit down very often, so these lazy episodes were a clubby rarity

We chattered and gossipped and lost track of time, content for the moment with life and each other, glad to be sharing Mother's rare leisure in our fleeting adolescent days.

Mother, in a loose-fitting, sleeveless housedress, sat like a flapper, with one leg thrown idly over the arm of the upholstered chair, her carefree, young position very unlike the style of her prim predecessors. Martha and I, with our tan, young legs also thrown over the chair arms, lounged slim and callow in white shorts and bright halters.

The three of us were as much alike on those indolent summer mornings as we were to ever be again.

We weren't old enough yet to resist or resent Mother's intrusions into our choices, nor were we able to guess that we would one day do a little intruding of our own. We weren't able to see much beyond what was then still a daisy chain of days.

We listened with continued interest to Mother's repeated tales of all-day trips in a rented fringed surrey from Twenty-first Street clear out to Ginger Hill, which belonged then to her father's father, Charles Erswell. It was all of seven miles, but back then it was a lush, picnic basket laden, big-deal-of-a-day with Grandpa Charles. He was charmed by Edna and her brother Chester, with their high spirits, their blond curls, and their appealing ways.

Growing up in the shadow of nothing, with no imposing blue hills or valleys, no majestic mountains in the distance or moving panoramic vistas for backdrops to our stage, with just flat Ohio farmland wherever you looked, where you couldn't see beyond the next house in town, and the sun seemed to set behind the drug store two blocks west, you can understand why Ginger Hill seemed greater than it was.

Today Ginger Hill backs up to a suburban development of new homes and faces onto a heavily trafficked thoroughfare (Alexis Road). But in those days, Aunt Iona tells me, it was a hill in an open country where there were no hills. To me it's still my great-grandfather's hill, and every time I pass it, which I often do, I see little phantom children in quaint little outfits, clambering its brambled sides, picking berries and running free in the wild grasses of its history.

We would giggle with dismay as Mother would tell how, as a young girl, she would often walk home from school backwards because she was embarrassed over her "fat" legs and didn't want anyone checking them out from behind. Actually, her legs were very pretty, but her story caused me to double-check my own, just in case I needed to walk home backwards too.

Are those "fat" legs?

With my growing addiction to all things sweet, I especially loved to hear Mother tell of how her mama would spend every Saturday filling the kitchen counter with pies and breads and coffeecakes and sweet rolls and devil's food cake, enough to last the entire week ahead. That's just the way they did it then. And then her mother would make tiny jam tarts out of leftover dough for the kids. So did my mama, and so did I. That kind of counter laden abundance—sinful, destructive and glorious—remains a secret goal of mine.

Martha and I would rattle on, interrupting and correcting each other, talking about school and friends and boys and plans, and Mother would laugh and question and nod and frown, quick to take our side in any imagined or real situation. I don't think that's necessarily good, but we were *her girls*, and we never doubted her love and acceptance. If anyone ever slighted us, and she knew about it, she never forgot it, although we did.

She talked about her old boyfriends and who she nearly married and who she didn't, and how and why she liked this one or that one, and how come Daddy was special. At thirteen and fifteen, this was the good part.

We'd listen again with undiminished fascination to the tragic tale of her baby brother, Chester. No matter how many times she told it, we were always fascinated, and no matter how many times I told it to my kids, they were always fascinated.

Her attitudes and values clung to her sentences. I recall her sympathy and her judgment, her warmth, tenderness, and rigidity. We took it all in, still too young to question much. Still looking to her for all the answers we didn't even know yet that we wanted or needed. It was a classroom, wasn't it?

The morning would wane, and the noonday heat would sneak indoors and take us by surprise.

Then suddenly Mother'd jump up and get moving. Her Billie Burke-like manner did not conceal a highly organized efficiency. Both Martha and I have her ability to accomplish a lot in short periods of time and her tendency to move annoyingly fast. Mother would head for the kitchen, grab some lemons, and have the aluminum shaker full of lemonade in a thrice. Then she'd give the pickles ripening in the iceroom crock a few good stirs, put the jelly jars waiting on the counter into the dishpan and then boil them on the stove in preparation for the grape jam to come, fix lunch with our help, make a pie for dinner, and get us started on the ironing.

She'd bang pots and pans around and laugh and say, "Bridget's in the kitchen" and "No rest for the wicked" and "It's a great life if you don't weaken." But it was all said lightly, and she never missed a beat.

And lots of the time she sang. And so did Daddy.

They both sang. A lot. With their feet on the ground.

As I grew older, I didn't always give Mother enough credit. Since she didn't read much and didn't seem curious enough for a curious daughter, I sometimes underestimated the commonsensical wisdom that she and Daddy poured over my life.

Here's one example. One day she did something especially wonderful for me. I learned then about the power of language to move and change things.

The Kellers lived across the street and owned a Dodge. It was 1936. The hood ornament on the car was a little chromium-plated goat, reared up on its back legs. My friend Lois crocheted a tiny rose-colored sweater for the goat. I thought this was pretty cute, and I told my father, who also thought it was pretty cute. So he had the *Sunday Times* photographer go out and take Lois's picture, with her crochet hook poised in her hand near the goat in the artificial way of newspaper photos. Daddy laid out the Sunday rotogravure section, and he put Lois's picture in a large oval in the middle of the front page.

The the Chrysler Corporation saw the picture and sent word for the whole Keller family to come to Detroit on the then new and fancy Mercury train for a day on the town.

When Lois got home, she came over and passed around the biggest box of chocolates (gift from Chrysler) I'd ever seen. We each took a piece. Lois left and I burst out crying.

Mother asked me to come and sit down at the dining room table with her. It was in the afternoon, and I think it was in the spring. I'm not sure. The tan window shades were drawn halfway down the windows, and I remember sitting down petulantly and staring at the golden color of the halfdrawn shades while my mind ran slides of Lois's box of chocolates.

Sadly, I don't remember any specifics of what Mother said, but what she said affected my whole life. She talked about jealousy and explained to me why I was crying over Lois's box of candy. Somehow, some way, long before Freud and Gesell and Spock hit the streets, she was able to make me understand my feelings in a way that freed me from the burden of one of life's most damaging spoilers. Jealousy has played virtually no role in my life, except for when I was on the receiving end of it in junior high school.

When we were just little girls, Martha and I sometimes wore coveralls in the morning, but every afternoon in summer we'd take cool baths and put on freshly pressed dresses, often still warm from the iron, and with the pleasant odor of near-scorch.

I've never gotten over missing that vanished ritual.

"Little Joan" and I would sometimes decide to take our baths at the same time, and we would yell to each other back and forth across the driveway, reporting as to our progress—"Now I'm washing my right foot," etc. Before long, we'd both appear in our front yards, looking and feeling and smelling like brand-new little 1930 girls, which we were.

Mother's sashaying-early-in-the-day demeanor quieted down too in the lemony afternoons. She would change from a simple cotton housedress to an "afternoon" dress of eyelet or dimity, often with a lacy white collar, which Daddy liked so much. (He always said that white collars set off a face and were flattering, and I think he was right.) On certain special afternoons, we'd walk with her to the drug store (down near where the sun set by the little Kroger store two blocks west) to get a chocolate soda. I remember sitting there at the tiny round marble table with my first straw in my mouth and chocolate waiting at the other end and not knowing how to use it. It only took one remark for me to quickly command a technique that despite behavior modification therapy, will not be denied.

Mother in a dimity dress, on a lemony afternoon

On other afternoons, with the potato salad waiting in the refrigerator, the tomatoes sliced, the beets cooling, and the chocolate pudding and ice tea at the ready, Mother would go out to sprinkle the front lawn, waiting till Daddy got home. I would watch her swinging the hose back and forth in exaggerated arcs, like the young girl she really still was, and watch her expression as the sun caught in the arcing spray and made transitory rainbows. Then she'd give me a turn at making rainbows and at squirting the dog.

The picture of Mother's easy grace as she stood there, the sense of her contentment with her role as she hummed and sprinkled, entered into my psyche and influenced my future.

Chapter 15

*Kindliness precedes psychiatry
by hundreds of years.*
—V.H.E.

I remember a raw, windy spring afternoon. Pinkie Lennex and I were about four then. We were standing, dressed in heavy sweaters, on the small terrace in front of his house. Pinkie was wearing a little leather helmet, popular with young aviators then.

His mother, Nellie, had just scolded him and, in a mindless outburst probably not uncommon with parents back in those days before we took Freud seriously, told him she was going to send him to an orphanage! A paralyzing threat to a child. We all knew what orphans were. I remember how awestruck I was every Sunday when we drove by the forbidding red brick building of St. Anthony's Orphanage on Cherry Street on our way to my grandma's house. I nearly pulled a neck muscle every Sunday looking for orphans in the windows. So I was almost as scared as Pinkie was.

At that exact moment, a small green truck, with a boxy wire enclosure in back, pulled to a stop in front of Pinkie's house. *How fast they had come for him!* We knew it had to be an orphange truck (with that little jail in back) come to pick up a naughty boy.

Actually it was a mail truck, which quickly moved on, the driver unaware of the anguish that his momentary intrusion into our neighborhood had caused. I doubt that Pinkie remembers the incident today. Probably not, since we all remember or repress according to our tolerance for pain.

Nellie never meant to frighten her little son. She just didn't think. Yet Pinkie grew up to be a fine man. But so many people carry wounds, psychic bruises, which sometimes never heal. In those days, the ignorance of psychology made children vulnerable to callous remarks. Those of us who emerged in relatively good shape can bless the luck of the parental draw (and our chemistry).

Isn't it sad that little children are so often at the mercy of impulsive, unknowing, or unthinking adults. It is one of life's sweetest (and luckiest!) blessings that most people love children and try to do what's best for them. Some are just better at it. Some don't care enough, but few are heartless.

I learned a lot from the people who lived on our block on Overland Parkway. Every family contributed something to what each of us became.

The parents included a dentist, a government employee, several salesmen, a doctor, an artist, a butcher, a gas station manager, and a group of hard-working mothers whose workday ran from 7 A.M. to midnight.

We had more than our share of bright kids; we were nearly all in the A class. There was a retarded boy around the corner and there was a tomboy and a sissy or two and a couple of brains and a cast of American regulars who I remember fondly.

The differing family styles on our street provided the kids with such contrasts. We took it all in, and what we saw became as much a part of us as the lilacs and the horses.

Andy and Tillie Tillotson, next door to us to the north in that "house of ever-changing neighbors," provided a contrast to the rest of the people on the block. They had no children and no pets. There were other ways in which they didn't fit with their neighbors.

They were friendly and young, and given to bursts of loud laughter and crude talk. Tillie was plump and pretty, and lots of times she wore a red beret tilted sharply to one side of her head. She had a coarse laugh which would ring out and cause Mother and Daddy to exchange glances. Then Martha and I would exchange glances. Then all four of us would exchange glances.

Once Tillie told mother that she (Tillie) had fallen "on her can," and Mother told Daddy. Next thing you know, Tillie was using the word *"tits"*. Now we were getting into big league shock stuff. Mother's horrified reaction on this one has stuck with me. Fifty years later I'm still able to duplicate it. And I do.

Except for their language, Mother and Daddy seemed to like the Tillotsons, and they joked back and forth across their porches until the conversations ended abruptly when one of the Tillotsons would holler out a crude assessment of something or other.

One summer afternoon when I was maybe three, I was standing in Tillotson's gravel driveway (no one *else* had a gravel driveway) when Andy suddenly came roaring into the driveway in his black Model T coupe. I froze in place. Andy jumped out of the car, swooped me into his arms, and carried me over into my own yard. The act was so full of gentle good humor and affection that I remember it still.

They never had kids. They never fit in. They never even tried. They just moved away. And I never saw them again, but I hope that they moved someplace where their warmth mattered more than their language.

I ought to have learned from them that language really shouldn't matter, but it didn't work out that way. The language of today's kids stands my hair on end, and it all started way back then when Tillie fell on her can.

Two of the mothers on the block were as different as their names, . . . Nellie and Emma. I never knew another Nellie or another Emma, but I'm sure that I'd know one if I saw one.

Quiet and steady Emma Keller

Emma Keller, with her tall, shapeless, sleeveless, housedresses, seemed to have brought the quiet, seasonal rhythm of the farm with her. She moved slowly, smiling, never hurried, as if she knew—like nature, like the good earth, like spring planting—that things would happen in their own good time. (Nobody ever told me about that!) I was always amazed that there was no sense of urgency in their home the way there was in ours.

Emma and her tall, boyish-looking husband, Arthur, were displaced farm people from Oak Harbor, and they led an orderly, church-going, chicken-on-Sunday, wash-on-Monday ("Did your mother wash today?") kind of life. No sparks flew from their house, and though they smiled a lot and were pleasant neighbors, we sensed a certain Lutheran disapproval coming across to our less staid side of the street.

In contrast, pert-nosed Nellie Lennex, a vivacious near-flapper, in strappy sandals and sassy hats, had her hair done in a beauty parlor (unheard of!) and hugged and kissed her big-lug-of-an-affable-traveling-salesman-husband near the kitchen window above the sink where we could see, and did.

The Lennexes in 1933,
with affable Dick smiling on his family

A lighthearted communion crisscrossed the driveway between our house and the Lennex home. Nellie and Mother gossipped and giggled over the back fence like girls, while Mite and Peggy barked at each other and touched noses through the wire mesh.

But then one day we all realized that big Dick Lennex (the neighborhood whistler) didn't look quite so big. And then on an August night in 1937, years before his family could get ready, he died of cancer. But not before he left a cheerful mark on his children and the rest of us.

On a rainy noontime when I was in the fourth grade, I hurried home from school for lunch, breathless with important adult information.

"Billy Nunemaker's mother died!" I panted to Mother who was standing by the stove.

Her face crumbled, and she reached for me, hugging me up against her bibbed apron. She began to cry. I thought about how we didn't know Mrs. Nunemaker all that well (she lived across the street). I wondered why Mother was so upset.

It was many years before I was to understand that she was crying for all the world's little lost babes, denied their mothers too soon. (Mrs. Nunemaker had died shortly after the birth of their third son.)

On that rainy noontime I was beginning to learn for the first time about sorrow that was not my own, . . . to feel someone else's pain. I felt the stab of my mother's tears for the Nunemaker's grief. My self-preoccupation began that day to melt away from my center. It was a beginning.

I wonder if those Overland Parkway twigs were bent in ways very different from today's twigs. Psychology was in its infancy back in the twenties and thirties and was certainly not in general use. It wasn't until 1893 that Freud first began to concentrate on patients' dreams in order to reach their inner selves. Many years were to pass before psychology caught the attention of parents. Common sense, intuition, contemporary social parameters and, of course, guilt were the only tools they had. Parents just plunged ahead, dealing moment to moment, pretty much in the imperfect style of their own parents, making lots of the same mistakes.

Some of us were lucky and some of us weren't.

Around one house in our neighborhood, the atmosphere often vibrated with screaming as the mother frequently spanked her two small children. Whenever we heard loud or prolonged crying, we kids would exchange uneasy glances. We would know at once who was screaming, and we could identify with the small behinds on the receiving end of an angry switch. We didn't know we were listening also to the possible sound of little psyches being damaged.

As we approached junior high, the younger of the two kids (he was in my room at school) would rise in daily mortification to take his turn at the blackboard. He would walk self-consciously and reluctantly up the aisle while all eyes focused on the darkened wet seat of his whistling corduroy knickers. His empty wooden desk seat was bleached down to the natural wood and was the object of much curiosity. An obvious odor trailed the damp corduroys, but I don't remember ever hearing anyone make overt fun of him. We must have been old enough to sympathize, and I don't remember the earlier years of his problem.

In recollection, recently, Meyer, a sensitive friend who shared those school days with me, recalled: "I remember one day in school how he (youngest son) suddenly buried his face in his arithmetic book. His cheeks flushed scarlet while under the seat, it went drip, drip, drip."

We both laughed at the description, but just as quickly exchanged looks of pained sympathy for the frequently spanked little boy who grew, perhaps inevitably, into a window peeking flasher in his teens.

My mother happened to see him one autumn afternoon as he dashed home from high school on his bicycle. Mother was curious over his haste as he hurled his bike against his house. In seconds she saw him in an upstairs bedroom window, just in time to present a little frontal nudity to educate the girls (including me) who spilled out of the three-thirty bus from DeVilbiss High School.

The word "sissy" was bandied about freely in those days, and I would guess it stung many a young boy who may have simply been more sensitive than other boys his age.

Today we would use a different word for the bright, darkly handsome neighbor boy who spent long hours with Martha and me drawing paper doll dresses. A passion of fashion designing consumed numberless summer afternoons in our cool basement recreation room. We designed dresses, bathing suits, entire luxurious wardrobes for the latest seven-inch paper doll, which had appeared the week before in the funnies section of the *Toledo Sunday Times* next to the "Tillie the Toiler" comic strip. Because Daddy was an artist, we had an advantage over other kids, with our large supplies of colored pencils and watercolors and various kinds of paper.

Our friend was very imaginative. We enjoyed his company and admired his designs. Early on, he set the avant-garde tone of our work when he colored an evening gown pink and black. It was a stunning innovation. One day we stared in fascination as he cut out a paper canoe and then cut horizontal slits in it. Next he cut small pillows, which he colored and placed in the slits. He then placed our currently favorite paper doll at a stiff angle against the pillows. Well! We were enchanted. Our imaginations rocketed us to Hollywood!

We never questioned his interest. But Daddy did. I remember overhearing Daddy say to Mother one afternoon when he returned from work, "Edna, will you get that damn pansy out of the basement!"

Actually, Daddy liked the boy with the soft dark eyes and the ready wit. But in those days of macho men and excessive role designation, he found it difficult to accept him as the paper-doll-drawing companion of his young daughters.

One summer, a country cousin came to visit the Kellers. Odessa was a big country girl, maybe twelve, several years older than her cousin Lois and me. I only saw her once. I remember she was wearing a gray-checked farm dress and standing on the curb across the street with Lois. I never have been able to erase her from my mind or forget that summer noontime.

A sparrow was pecking at horse manure in the street in front of us. Swift as a hawk, Odessa swooped down and grabbed the tiny sparrow in her hand. Just as swiftly and in a wild arcing motion, she hurled the bird to the pavement. The injured sparrow convulsed madly in the street. My heart, like a sparrow in my chest, fluttered madly too. I ran into the house for sanctuary, but it was too late.

Odessa, why did you do that to that little bird and to me?

Finally our generation began to grow up, and when we were first exposed to Freud and Psych 101, many of us were enthralled and infatuated. It was all so new. And we knew something our parents didn't know!

We began to take part in a great new hobby—the laying on of guilt as we sat in merciless judgment of our parents.

The Brave New World of the mind was upon us. *Analyze* was the *in* word. The air was crackling with change. All kinds of change.

While our minds were breaking free of the old ways of looking at things, the solid, predictable old ways of our neighborhood were changing too. The familiar faces we had watched coming and going, getting on and off the Eleanor bus, slamming doors, calling the kids home at dark, shovelling driveways, moving sprinklers, going to vote, scolding, laughing, doing the same things day in and day out were changing.

The Depression which had denied us so much had also blessed us with the security of limits and repetition.

Today the neighborhood looks surprisingly the same, though the once-vacant lots aren't vacant anymore. New kids (little intruders) play jacks and marbles on the same warm sidewalks where we had scraped our knuckles.

It is starting all over again. Only an erupting volcano burying the city could stop the genesis, freeze the little intruders at their play, like Pompeians. Future archeologists would never know if it was us or them.

Most all of those eager, young 1920's parents, who remain so vividly in my mind, are gone. A few linger on, the McGrews, Nellie Lennex, and Arthur Keller. Nellie and Arthur are not aware that they are neighbors once more as they wait and wait in the Lutheran's Old Folks Home.

They struggle, and fail, to recognize the dear, vaguely familiar faces of the visiting children they once adored.

Chapter 16

Autumn catches us with our vocabularies down.

—V. H. E.

Back when there was a lot more time than money, our entertainment was usually homemade, like the fudge. Mostly it was a smattering of small, joyful things which we sprinkled over the ordinary days like bright confetti. Things like picnics and birthday parties and overnights at friends' and trips into our imaginations. Sometimes we'd go places for paid entertainment, but mostly during the Depression we had to rely on ourselves. We didn't have money, and we didn't have television.

Each season dictated what we would do. When autumn would come in moodily, we would rake leaves into leaf houses and inhale the sharp, spicy tang of chili sauce drifting from the still-open windows of the neighborhood kitchens where our mothers had spent August and September filling clear blue Mason jars with peaches and pickles and chili sauce. The smell of the cooking sauce would mix with the tang in the air and, forever after, the sight and smell of chili sauce, unexpected in a cut-glass dish, would send me back through time to those first, frosty, unforgettable autumn days.

We would scuff home from school through the smoke-filled shafts of sunlight and rush to change into play clothes. Then we'd play statue and hurl each other into piles of leaves. And the boys would stuff handfuls of leaves down the backs of the girls' sweaters. When we went home to supper, we'd take off our sweaters and rain leaves throughout our mothers' tidy houses.

After supper, we would burn leaves at the curbs in the smoky darkness. Sometimes a burning leaf would be caught in an updraft of

My fifth birthday party, September 20, 1929;
I'm sitting in the front, fourth from the right.

wind, and it would become a swirling art object, flaming upward in the night sky with our eyes in tow.

My asthma would let up with the first frost. I could breathe again, and the season so dazzled me that I fell in love and never got over it. On clear October days I still feel like Blanche DuBois when she said, "Oh, sometimes there's God . . . so quickly."

Sometimes in the autumn Daddy would stand in the open front door and look up at the night sky and the haunting moon for a long quiet time. Then he'd sing "Shine On, Harvest Moon" softly to himself.

One Halloween, when I was about eight, we had an orange pasteboard jack-o'-lantern that held a burning candle on top of our living room table. I was doing homework in a chair and Mother's mama, who was staying with us at the time, was sitting opposite me in her favorite Cogswell chair (and it was Peggy's favorite too). With no outward change of expression, she called "Edna" in a thin, reedy voice (Mother was upstairs). "Edna," she repeated quietly. She didn't move or gesture. Before I could yell "Mother!" for her (I didn't know *why* she was calling), Daddy appeared from upstairs and, in a sudden rush, dashed past us to what was now a jack-o'-lantern and our big living room table lamp next to it engulfed in flames. I jumped up in alarm. Daddy grabbed the lamp, rushed to the front door, and hurled the lamp into the darkness and into the arms of Stanley Sullivan (Julia's father), who happened to be passing by and saw the flames in our window. Stanley arrived on our porch at the same time the lamp arrived. No one was hurt, and Mama never got out of her chair. After that, Daddy often wondered aloud just what it would take for Grandma "to get the lead out."

Coasting at Willys Park; I'm on top.

In the winter, after school, we coasted at Willys Park until we couldn't feel our feet anymore in the ice-blue afternoons. And sometimes in the evening we went sledding down the meager little slope of Overland Parkway, north of Eleanor Avenue, while the new falling snow made the streetlights all fuzzy and turned the neighborhood into a Bavarian village with cottony roofs and frosty yellow windows. Then we'd bring our temperatures back to normal by going home and drinking cups of hot cocoa with oozy marshmallows.

One day when I was ten or eleven, Mother told me that I was *not* to go coasting in my brand-new snowsuit under any circumstance. A circumstance arose the very next day that I couldn't refuse, and I went to Willys Park with the other kids to coast.

In my memory, believe it or not, this was the first time I so blatantly disobeyed my parents. That's just the way it was with most kids then.

On my first trip down the hill, I fell off the sled and discovered to my horror that I had torn a triangle in my new snowpants. Mother always said that a triangle was the hardest tear to mend.

I walked the ten cold blocks home in the dwindling winter daylight, dawdling in apprehension. I took my time, noticing the silhouettes made by the houses and the trees as the sun slipped low and orange behind them. I studied the snowy details, the long blue shadows, the voluptuous drifts, the glinting icicles. When I got home, I crept in the back door and down to the laundry room to take off my snowy clothes. I lingered there in the near darkness, trying to figure out what to tell Mother.

After supper, we went in the living room to listen to Lux Radio Theater. I sat down next to Mother on the davenport, and she began fussing with my hair in that annoying way that mothers do. Warmed by her affection, I blurted out my story. To my astonishment, Mother started to cry. I sat up startled and began to spill apologies. But she didn't act angry. She didn't even scold me. She didn't need to. Unsettled by her continuing tears, and ashamed, I began to cry too. She put her arms around me.

There we sat. I was crying because I had made my mother cry, and Mother was crying over all the dozens of accumulated little crises of the Depression.

I know now that she was crying over the long hours that Daddy had spent to earn that brown wool snowsuit with the yellow and orange trim, hours spent over a drawing board at night while his neck ached and his eyes burned. She was also crying for all the things that she and Daddy did without so they could put their daughters into warm coats and sweet dresses. Like most of the world's parents, they didn't mind doing without. Except sometimes.

Daddy drawing a forest background for an imp

When Ohio's reluctant spring would finally come, we'd put on our shorts too soon and break out the jump rope ("Teddy Bear, Teddy Bear, go upstairs. Teddy Bear, Teddy Bear, say your prayers. . . .") and play marbles by the hour ("sitting on the damp ground," our mothers would say) in the vacant lot. We'd horn in on the boys' baseball games and sail toothpicks in the leftover rainwater rushing along the curbs on April afternoons. We'd study the tulips and daffodils and bugs and all the other first things of spring, so new to us who were also new. We'd sit on our porch steps, and I'd show the kids how Daddy would make "frogs" out of live-forever plant leaves. And we'd blow iridescent soap bubbles from white clay pipes. We'd eat lunch in the backyard and end the day singing popular songs from pastel song sheets the size of newspaper pages, which we bought for a nickel at the drug store.

And sometimes on a spring evening when the kids had all been called home, I'd stay out on the front steps in the mysterious darkness and look up at the sky, and I'd wonder and wonder and wonder. And I still do.

Suddenly it would be summer, mad with the sound of crickets and lawnmowers and June bugs and Marcie Keller screaming before her afternoon nap (every day) and Jimmie Keller mechanically pounding out "The Parade of the Wooden Soldiers" on their upright piano (every day).

Geraniums bloomed in window boxes up and down the block, and the indoors and the outdoors would become one.

One summer we rented a cottage at Clark's Lake in Michigan (twenty-five dollars per week). I was five. I was thrilled to have our own cottage, just down the road from Julia's. I remember late one afternoon I was dreamily paddling around in shallow water, floating in an old black inner tube, trailing my hands and feet and bottom in the water. The lake felt so warm, and the sun was dropping low in the sky, making the surface of the water look slippery and orange. I felt so happy. Everything was just exactly right.

Then . . .

The inntertube had a blowout! This was my first experience with terror. It was the first time I ever walked on water, heading back to the cottage and Mother's arms.

Summer was always a time of strong sensations, when our young bodies were exposed to the sun and wind and bumble bees and skinned knees and tetanus shots and sunburn. The closed-in, bundled-up seasons had slipped away so unceremoniously. The high point in most summers came when we headed for our two-week vacation on Traverse Bay in northern Michigan.

Teamwork was necessary to pack up a 1930 Hudson with two kids and a dog and a couple of inner tubes, and virtually no trunk space. The running board had to be utilized, and rope held us altogether.

Our 1930 Hudson took us up to Traverse Bay in Michigan.

Martha and I were small enough to allow for stacked-up boxes on half of the back floor. The top box was filled with little tissue-wrapped gifts, which we were allowed to open as we arrived in Ann Arbor! Flint! Bay City! Standish! Clare! Gaylord! and Elk Rapids! That box remains one of my favorite summer memories.

A high priority space was left on the back floor for Peggy. If she didn't have floor space, she threw up.

Departure time was the mood-altering, cobalt-blue hour of 5:30 A.M. By then, Mother and Daddy had packed and repacked several times, checked the stove twice, checked the water heater, and stopped arguing over how to pack and repack.

Martha and I, excited but sleepy, clambered eagerly into the blanket-covered, pillow-laden, inviting back seat. Peggy, trembling for fear of being left behind, curled up in her space and went into a seven-hour coma. But she always threw up at least once.

Finally all was ready, and we drove off into the first tender light of morning. Magic, dressed in a summer suit, jumped into the car with us, and a feeling akin to Christmas Eve settled like dew over the boxy green car. We tootled along U.S. 23 and, as quickly as you could say "Queen Anne's Lace," we were deep in the Michigan countryside.

Daddy didn't say, "Sit up and observe" this time, because he was hoping we would fall asleep. He wouldn't have needed to anyhow, for Martha and I were sleepily peeping over the back window sills, taking in all the drowsy farm scenes, the mist rising like mystery from farm ponds, and the cows, dozing in the wet grasses, snugly close to the big red Michigan barns.

We felt alone and complete, with everything we cared about packaged and tied up and moving along as a unit in a sweet and sleeping world.

I gazed dreamily at Mother's and Daddy's blue silhouettes ahead of us in the car. First Daddy, in a low, mellow voice and then Mother, joining him in her familiar light croon, began to sing their litany of songs, lullaby-soft and anesthetizing. "Won't you come over to my house. . . ." "Take me out to the ball game. . . ." and "Hello, Central . . ." were all sung as we drove north.

Peggy was my constant playmate, until we both turned sixteen.

They were so young . . . and the car was so full of their plans and dreams and their love for the sleepy threesome in the back seat. It was the beginning of the thirties, and though so much was wrong with the world then, so much was right with the world then. There was no way for them to know that their financial ship would never arrive.

Their silhouettes grew vague and hazy as I drifted off into unfinished sleep. The Hudson did its part by rocking along like a cradle on wheels and not breaking down till we got to Fenton.

Bye bye blues! Bye bye blues!
Bells ring, birds sing,
Sun is shining, no more pining;
Just we two . . .

"m-m-m-m-m m-m-m-m-m
m-m-m-m-m"
"z-z-z-z-z z-z-z-z-z z-z-z-z-z"

When we woke up in Bay City, Mother realized that the chocolate cake with the caramel frosting (another favorite of mine) had been left on the kitchen counter.

I was a long time getting over that.

Chapter 17

It's crazy when you think about it, how we used to sit around straining our eyeballs looking at the radio.

—Dick Eyster, author's husband

Jigsaw puzzles reached their zenith in the thirties when it became necessary to entertain ourselves inexpensively with home games like Monopoly and Parcheesi and Chinese checkers. But when dusk fell, radio ruled our world. Radios clicked on in every house up and down the block and up and down the land as families gathered for the day's shared respite from hard times.

The shows were mostly scary like "The Hermit" or "Fu Manchu" or "Omar the Wizard of Persia"; or they were funny like Joe Penner and Jack Benny and Fred Allen (our favorite), "Fibber McGee & Molly," "Baby Snooks," "Vic & Sade," "Charlie McCarthy" and endless other shows and serials like "Jimmie Allen," "Orphan Annie," and "Myrt & Marge."

Radios, art deco boxes of every size and shape, occupied a major place in our living rooms and in our lives. I especially loved the Friday nights back in the early days before hormonal changes in Martha and me and our school chums changed the face of everything.

There was a radio show on Friday nights which we waited for all week. It was called "The Little Theatre Off Times Square." There was a forgettable story each week, but the stars—Barbara Luddy and Les Tremaine and Jim Ameche—lured and lulled us with their mellow and honeyed radio-perfect voices. And they ignited our imaginations, spinning the ether waves into stage settings with dramatic moments and characters, all inside our heads.

Martha and I would turn out all the lights in the living room, except for the two small wall lamps above the mantel. The dim little lights transformed the living room into our own personal theatre. We finished making the popcorn just before the radio announcer cooed: "Smoking in the outer lobby only, please." And in a flash, we were in distant, glamorous New York City, with the sound of taxi horns and crowds in the background. We rushed to our chosen places, and an expectant hush fell over the room. Mother and Daddy humored our addiction by joining us and, I suspect, enjoyed it even more than we did because they were aware of the fleeting family togetherness. Mother brought in tumblers of homemade grape juice, culled from the lush and limited purple harvest behind the garage. And we all sat munching popcorn while Peggy drooled next to each one of us in turn.

As Martha and I grew older, and our sensibilities more tender, we became enchanted with the love stories on the show, especially as they dripped toward the inevitable conclusions. At the end, as Jim Ameche's voice dropped sensuously lower and lower, the lovers on the radio fell hungrily upon each other. At that sacred moment, Daddy would suddenly stand up and emit a loud raspberry or Bronx cheer. He was so predictable, yet Martha and I were always startled out of our reveries and always flagrantly furious. Daddy, delighted with his ability to puncture the moment week in and week out, would exit, doubled over laughing. Our anger was short-lived, and we were back at it the following Friday.

By 1940, Martha and I were both dating on weekends, and we left Mother and Daddy behind, listening to "The Little Theatre Off Times Square" and perpetuating something which had ended for their daughters.

Meanwhile, for sheer day-in and day-out, season-in and season-out peak entertainment, nothing could light our fires like the movies. With their glitter and glamor and surprises and shocks, they lifted us out of our spartan lives and into worlds we could never have seen or known about otherwise. They still do. They were such a big deal. They *are* such a big deal.

We spent so many Saturdays and Sundays standing in long lines, with a dime in our hot little hands, at the neighborhood Westwood Theatre down at the corner of Sylvania Avenue and Belmar. Shirley Temple was my first obsession. I made scrapbook after scrapbook of her twinkling pictures. But it wasn't long before the moon-washed love scenes of Jeanette MacDonald and Nelson Eddy, singing "When I'm Calling You-Ooo-Ooo-Ooo-Ooo-Ooo-Ooo" into each other's wide-open mouths, edged Shirley onto the siding.

Today, the old Westwood still stands at Sylvania and Belmar, its attractive 1930 stone facade now cheapened by a plastic marquee gasping out erotica. Every time I drive by, I see, through a glass darkly, the lingering ghosts of Shirley and Jeanette, and I long for our dear, dead innocence.

For me, the sweetest deal of all was getting cleaned up and going downtown on the bus with Mother to meet Daddy. On those evenings we'd go to the palatial Paramount Theatre. In spite of his free passes, we felt like royalty.

The sparkle that was Paris and the glory that was Rome was just seven miles away and a nickel ride from home

The *Greyhound,* a big Lake Erie pleasure boat that plied the waters between Toledo and Cedar Point in the thirties, came close, in intensity, to eclipsing our two-week summer vacation.

The pleasure steamer Greyhound

Oh! what a beautiful morning when we woke on the day of the cruise and marched smartly down to the Madison Avenue dock with a full picnic basket. Standing in the crowd, in the huge shadow thrown on the dock by the big boat, we kids would dart about like spilled marbles, keeping a mindful eye on our mothers, who were standing at the ready by the gangplank. I would study the scary waters lapping mysteriously around the dock pilings and would study the thick, wet ropes. For all my life, because of family stories, I was terrified of deep water. Breathing the still-cool morning air, laced with the smell of marine life, I would feel near to bursting with the rare feeling of adventure. Year in and year out, parents and kids alike seized upon this summer experience. It was as close as most of us were ever going to come to adventure at sea.

The muddy water of the Maumee River, which long, long before had sparkled in the cupped hands of kneeling Ottawa Indians, was already thickening with sludge in 1934. The ancient meandering river, the largest to flow into the Great Lakes, was heading inexorably toward the total pollution of the 1970s.

At departure time, we exploded onto the boat and disappeared for the day, scurrying among the couples on the dance floor, dashing up and down the narrow stairs, and touching base with our mothers and their baskets only occasionally. We ran from one end of the exotic ship to the other, all the luxurious, hungered-for day long. And our mothers felt joy in our joy, freedom in our freedom, and youth in our youth. This, they thought, was what summer and motherhood were all about: happy children, running free in the open air and out of sight most of the time.

On the lower deck were several coin-machine games. One was a glass case which enclosed the upper half of a mysterious black-clad, bejewelled gypsy lady. Her disturbing, but sightless, eyes stared out of a waxen face. When we inserted a nickel, the machine began to grind, and the lady's arms began to move in slow motion as she attempted (and repeatedly failed) to pick up valuable (cheap junk) prizes scattered in the case and to drop them down an opening for our retrieval. We watched in dismay as she inexplicably dropped the "diamond-encrusted" watch *every* time. Who among us was the daring one who discovered that the gypsy lady continued to reach for prizes when we inserted Necco candy wafers into the machine? I remember one time that we Neccoed all day and never won a darn thing. We got what was coming to us. . . . nothing. But the candy concessionaire must have made a killing on Necco sales.

The *Greyhound* could have been the *QE2* for all we kids knew. She thrilled us and exhausted us and offered us a major diversion in a summer full of days.

By the time we eased into the Madison Avenue dock at the end of the day, we were nautical veterans. Frazzled and dazzled, we walked on sealegs back to where Daddy waited for us in the steamy Hudson, his tie loosened, his straw skimmer hat tilted back on his head above his ruddy, overheated cheeks. Heat was still falling out of the sky, and we were asleep in the back seat before we were halfway home.

Mother and Daddy went to frequent costume parties in those days. They were usually given by the Art Klan or other art organizations to which Daddy belonged. The artists enjoyed the creativity of costume designing, and Mother was Daddy's willing and able recruit as a seamstress.

One memorable design was for a Dutch boy and girl. It was made of oil cloth. Mother dyed floor mops yellow and orange for the wigs, and this resulted in a scary lifetime dream for me. I was five years old. I remember I was lying in bed, when in the pale light of dreams, the Dutch boy's head, resplendent in floor-mop hair, appeared frighteningly in my window. In magic dream fashion, he kidnapped me and, running through dream wind to the backyard down at the corner, he hung me, dream-style, by my collar on the neighbor's clothesline where I have twisted slowly in the wind for fifty-five years. I have no notion why the dream returns to me so often, but it is the only one that does.

Mother and Daddy's costumes for the Art Klan Masque.

One unusual, exciting, and temporary entertainment that we loved had a very short life. No one I know, except my husband, remembers it.

It was truly an invention from a vanished time, lived and nearly forgotten forever.

In an open field somewhere in West Toledo in 1929 or 1930 (and it may have been for only two summers) stood a large wooden structure, not unlike a roller coaster, built as a ride for family automobiles (it was before the days of liability insurance). The trick and the treat was for fathers to drive their families up and down the rolling wooden hills. The excitement for kids was just incredible. I adored that thing.

I think today's overdosed children would be just as excited as we were.

Many summer days were spent drawing in our basement. When I wasn't staring in the icebox or messing around outdoors, I was drawing, or copying, pictures out of magazines like *Collier's* and *Esquire*. I would draw for hours and hours, and Martha often did too. Daddy saw to it that we had art lessons every Saturday morning at Keane's Art School and later at the museum. The beauty of the museum and its contents filled up my senses at an early age. Mr. Keane had been dean of the Chicago Art Institute when Daddy had gone there, so he only charged Daddy a dollar a lesson for us. Those lessons were a unique experience in arts vérité and exposure to a gentlemen of unusual culture.

By the time I was in junior high, I was getting serious crushes on artists. I wrote to Earl Cordrey and Jon Whitcomb and George Petty. I was thrilled when Mr. Cordrey sent me an original drawing. I touched it and ran my fingers over the pen lines and studied the unattainable skill.

The Petty girl in *Esquire* magazine quickly became a phenomenon because she was as risqué as anything ever got in those days. The girls were unreal—fetching and pert-bosomed, with hefty, curvaceous legs in high heels, and often filmy gowns.

Today the filmy gown has been replaced with total frontal and rearal and upside-downal nudity.

And the movies, too. Sigh.

And now there's MTV to add to the emotional malformation that I believe is undoubtedly taking place in today's kids. It really scares me.

I wish I could take them all back to Overland Parkway for a shot of good old-fashioned innocence.

Chapter 18

. . . . the pain and the glory and the heartbreak at the heart of things.

—John Hall Wheelock
"Dear Men and Women"

Every family has collections of stories and anecdotes, which are passed down from generation to generation with humor or tenderness or sadness.

Often the old family tales are just simple or personal brief episodes, but they illuminate a moment or a trait or an embarrassment or a fleeting triumph that is in danger of being forgotten forever.

In the lamplight of memory, these moments tie us to our past, help us get acquainted with those with whom we share a blood link. The stories belong to us alone, until we begin to share them with others.

"HE HAD A DREAM" (First Tale)

As children, we were fascinated and horrified by Mother's tale of a summer vacation gone tragically awry.

The story begins in 1913. It starts with a young boy's dream. He is fifteen. My mother's family consisted of three sisters and two brothers, growing older with a widowed mother (Mama May) in a roomy house on Twenty-second Street in Toledo. Mother's father had died in "that insane asylum" out on South Street when she was ten, and Mama was left to support her five children as a seamstress, with the help of Iona.

The house was often shared by numerous unmarried aunts and uncles who came and went as the vicissitudes of life swept them along.

That spring, visitors arrived for an overnight stay. The family's baby brother, Chester (the sunny, lively, doted-upon constant companion of my mother's baby days, since they were just a year and a half apart in age and looked like cherubim and seraphim according to their older sister, Alma), was obliged to give up his bed to accommodate the visitors.

Chester Charles Erswell in 1898 age 2 1/2,
he is wearing a navy blue velvet suit made by his mother, Hermina.
At 15, he had a premonitory dream of his own death by drowning.

Chester had turned fifteen in the spring of that year, and his handsome young features were giving way to a heavier, more manly look. It was this face in transition that all were to look upon in horror in the rapidly approaching future.

The night on which Chester relinquished his bed for the guests, he shared his mother's room. It was during this night that he had the dream. Sometime during the hours toward dawn, he called out in his sleep that he was going to die in a certain number of days.

Grandmother took the dream seriously. People put a lot of stock in portents of the future in those days.

His mother tried to waken him. She tried to question her sleepy son, but he was fast asleep again. She lay wakeful and shaken in the darkness. She was certain he had said he was going to die in eighty-four days.

She enlisted the help of the older brother and sisters to be wary, to keep watch, to walk to and from school with her final fledgling. He was a sophomore at Scott High School.

Days and weeks and months passed. Still Grandmother remembered. Eighty-four days came and went. Slowly, very slowly, the dream began to fade. A year passed.

Summer 1914 arrived. The family planned, with mounting excitement, for a rare vacation, a week at Zuke Lake near Ann Arbor, Michigan. Mother often told us of the dramatic days of preparation, of the baking of bread and pies, of the rising anticipation as plans were made to include friends Helen and Carl, Roland and Albert.

My mother had just graduated from Scott, and her sister Alma had just earned a bachelor's and master's degree simultaneously from Oberlin College. It was a time for celebration. Spirits were high! Boyfriends were in boisterous attendance, and the atmosphere was light and happy!

Two hours later it was all over, the "vacation" had ended.

As is the natural wont of kids at a lake, Chester headed at once for the water and a canoe. Mother's high-school boyfriend, Roland Bemis, got into the canoe with him. They paddled out, unfamiliar with the rather treacherous aspects of the lake.

Grandmother (Mama) had inexplicably gone for a walk. Fate had removed her from the scene she had feared for so long.

No one was able to explain how it happened, but within moments the canoe tipped over above a severe drop-off in the lake, barely twenty feet from shore. Chester went under and never resurfaced. Aunt Iona, standing on the shore, rushed into the water, but was quickly pulled down by the weight of her linen dress. She was able to grab Roland, and the two of them were pulled back to shore.

No one could swim. The panicky family ran to the Neuhausel's cottage next door and jumped into their rowboat. An oarlock broke. More panic.

Finally, divers were summoned. Even they were unsuccessful. A vigil was kept through the night in a rowboat placed to guard a narrow channel which ran around behind the cottages to the "bottomless" Devil's Basin. It was feared that the current in the channel might carry Chester's body to the basin. Horror gripped the family.

In the morning they watched as grappling hooks were brought to the scene. Speculation was that Chester's clothing had caught on a submerged log. The next day, the lake was dynamited, and Chester's body rose to the surface. The grappling hooks had scratched a large cross on his pale young face.

A mortician from a nearby town curtained off one end of the cottage porch and did the embalming on the site because state law forbade taking an unembalmed body out of state.

The stunned family and friends returned home from the vacation that never was.

The adored baby brother, who had been moving inexorably toward manhood, stayed a baby brother forever. The whole of his young life was halted in the cool darkness at the bottom of a lake. No one was to know what he might have been, for he stayed behind while the others grew old.

Grandmother, remembering the dream, counted the days.

Three hundred and eighty-four.

QUICK-WITTED AND TRAGIC SHERMAN ERSWELL
(Second Tale)

Aunt Iona remembers a summer day in 1898. She was eight. The setting is the train station in Augusta, Missouri, which served the trains that ran alongside the Missouri River. Aunt Iona's father, Sherman Erswell (my maternal grandfather), was stationmaster, freight handler, telegrapher, and ticket seller.

Aunt Iona says that Augusta was often called "Little Germany" then, because everyone was German except her father and the high-school teacher. There was one two-room school: one room for high school, one room for grade school. The streets were mud and had no names. There was a hotel down by the train station named Wencker, and two general stores, one run by one of the Wencker boys. The population was five hundred, and the people were mostly farmers.

There wasn't much to do on a lazy summer day in Augusta except watch the trains come and go, in and out of town on a single track, carrying along with them the exciting feeling that there was actually something going on out there around the bend and beyond the bluffs and beyond the wide Missouri.

On this particular summer day, Aunt Iona left the big house built into the slope and meandered down the dirt road to the station to watch the train come in. She remembers clearly watching as her father flagged the train on. Somehow he was suddenly caught and pulled under the wheels. In horror, she watched several cars pass over him, and then fled in panic around behind the station so she could not see. When she reappeared, the train was out of sight and her father was standing on the platform, brushing off his clothes!

"Agile and quick-witted," she said; her father had managed to pull himself snugly into the middle of the track where no part of him could catch in the wheels.

Aunt Iona remembers how her sensitive younger brother, Little Bud, got a stomachache and cried one day when he looked below and saw a wrecked train because he thought the train was hurt.

Aunt Iona remembers how up the hill behind their house was still more hill—a hill with a door in it, and behind the door a regular room with dirt walls. The room was a storage cellar for food my grandmother grew on the hilltop, and it was also a storm cellar for Missouri tornadoes.

On the top of the hill to the right of the gardens was an outhouse. The same sensitive little Bud, when he was four, manipulated his two-year-old sister, my mother, to accompany him up to the toilet because he was afraid of spiders. It always backfired because Mother would say, "There's a fider," (scream from Bud), "There's anudder fider," (scream), and "There's a fider web" (scream).

Aunt Iona remembers another day at the station. She was watching a big man questioning her father, who was working the telegraph key in the little room that juts forward in old train stations so the telegrapher can see the trains coming and going. Hot-tempered anyway, and highly annoyed, my grandfather socked the persistent man through the unscreened window and flattened him.

Later in the day, the man went to report the incident to the town mayor. When my grandfather opened the door, the startled man said, "So you're the pugilist and the mayor too!"

Then my grandfather invited the wronged man in to dinner.

"Suddenly and erratically," says Iona, "the next year, in nineteen-hundred, my father moved the family to Toledo." Toledo was his father's home—great-grandfather Charles's, who had escaped from a southern prison during the Civil War.

Slowly, then quickly, her father's temper deteriorated into psychotic episodes of violent behavior. In 1901, in desperation, Mama had her handsome, young (age thirty-five) husband committed to the insane asylum. Aunt Iona was thirteen. She is now ninety-five, and she remembers the long South Avenue streetcar rides with her mother to visit him. She remembers it all.

He lived on there for ten long years, dying an undramatic and lonely death at age forty-five, mentally ill and tubercular.

Seventy years later, I stood in morning shadows on the same grounds where the grandfather I had never known had suffered so long. I was a counselor for troubled kids who were being schooled in a building where some of Toledo's erstwhile "insane" had been housed.

I felt so oddly emotional, such an unreasonable bond, such a sorrow for the sorrow of my mother's family and the helpless, hopeless man who lived and died there.

"A DEED SO FIENDISH . . ." (Third Tale)

My grandmother Julia's papa was named August Heck. He lived "in a dwelling" (farmhouse) at the corner of Bancroft and Wakeman (now Vermont), near downtown Toledo, in what was then open country.

In the early morning hours of June 1, 1869, when Julia was about four years old, "dear Papa" was shot by a neighbor.

The following story appeared in *The Toledo Commercial:*

Toledo Commercial.

WEDNESDAY MORNING, JUNE 2

SHOOTING AFFAIR.

Daring Attempt to Commit a Murder—Two
Shots Fired and Three Balls Take
Effect—Arrest of the
Guilty Party.

Philip Steinmetz, a laborer, residing on Hewey street, near Bancroft, and August Heck, a baker, lives at the corner of Bancroft and Wakeman streets, the dwellings of the two men being but a few rods distant from each other. One day last week, an un-

ruly cow belonging to Steinmetz, broke into the garden of Heck. The latter caught the cow and tied her up in his own yard, thinking to keep her until the owner would pay the damage which she had done. Steinmetz, however, went and got his cow, against the protestations of Heck, and drove her off without showing any disposition to settle for the damages. This somewhat enraged Heck who followed the owner of the cow as he drove her off and insisted upon payment for what had been destroyed by the unruly cow.

At about two o'clock yesterday morning Heck's family and some of his neighbors were aroused from their slumbers by the report of a gun-shot. Mrs. Heck at once told her husband that some person had shot into their front room. Steinmetz, it seems, brought Heck and his wife in the room fronting on Wakeman street, and had fired four balls from a shot gun through the window and curtain into the wall, on the opposite side of the room, about where he supposed they would take effect in the sleepers. Heck and his wife, fortunately, were sleeping in the middle room, having windows on Bancroft street.

When Heck's wife told him that some person had shot into the front room, he at once got out of bed and went up stairs to a window, directly over the one in his sleeping apartments, to see if he could discover what was the matter. In the meantime Steinmetz had gone back to his house and re-loaded the empty barrel. In about fifteen minutes from the time the first shot was fired, Heck saw Steinmetz coming along towards the house, from Hewey street, walking on the ground beside the sidewalk. He did not stop until he reached the window of the room where Heck slept. Heck was at the window but stood to one side to avoid being seen, merely putting his head far enough forward to see what Steinmetz was doing. He discovered the latter putting his gun into the window of his sleeping apartments when he spoke and asked him what he was doing there. Steinmetz stepped back but one or two paces and then fired at Heck. Four balls passed through the siding near the window through the lath and plaster and three of them struck Mr. H.

The wounds are not considered dangerous, but they are very painful and will necessarily disable Mr. H. for some time. The bones in the hand, we learn, were badly broken and it will probably be crippled.

Steinmetz is about 45 years of age, and has a wife, but no children. He has been esteemed a troublesome man by his neighbors, but had no quarrel with Heck until the one about the cow, which is detailed above

It is seldom that we are called upon to record a deed so fiendish in its character. His first shot was just as likely to kill the wife as the husband, or any other pe son who might have been sleeping in the room. It was simply an effort to kill or wound somebody, the author of the deed no doubt hoping the victim would be Heck. His going back home after the first shot, reloading the empty barrel, and then returning and making an effort to shoot in the window of the room in which Heck and his wife slept, showed a cool and deliberate purpose to commit a murder under circumstances of the most brutal and atrocious character. He did not kill his victim, hence the law will spare his life, though in reality a more guilty man never stretched a rope.

The officers found the shot gun used by Steinmetz at his house, with one barrel loaded and the other empty.

THURSDAY MORNING, JUNE 8

Local and Miscellaneous

Improving.—August Heck, the wounded man, was reasonably comfortable yesterday

Steinmetz.—This man, who attempted the murder of August Heck, was taken before Judge Cummings yesterday morning, and committed to jail to await an examination on Friday.

Died.—Mr. August Heck, shot by Philip Steinmetz on Tuesday morning last, an account of which was given in Wednesday's Commercial, died of lockjaw on Sunday forenoon. The Coroner's inquest will probably be concluded to-day. A post mortem examination has been made and we learn that the physicians will report to day that Mr. Heck died of lockjaw caused by his wounds.

He left behind what must have been a rather exceptional wife and three small children: Julia, Amelia, and Edward. Buried forever is the information about how the Widow Heck managed to rear her three little ones. Back in the days when women had so few options, she was forced to be extremely resourceful, and her babes grew into fine adults.

You know about Julia.

Edward became a successful and generous man, regularly gifting his sisters with clothing and jewelry and affection.

Large houses are not the only measure of one's success, but in Edward's case it marked his rise from difficult beginnings in a widowed home. He lived with his family in a large white house on Parkwood Avenue in Toledo's lovely Old West End.

His sister Amelia had an even larger house.

Grandmother Julia's sister, Amelia, married Christian Gerber; in 1872 they built what they deemed a "lavish country estate" on Collingwood Avenue in Toledo. It later became Mary Manse College and still stands today as one of Toledo's reminders of her Victorian glory.

Amelia Heck Gerber, Julia's sister

"ALAS, POOR ALMA!" (Fourth Tale)

Alma was the one of the five children in Mother's family about whom we heard the most and knew the least. We know that she had "a lovable disposition," and was artistic and bright. But I never knew her at all because she "disappeared" when I was only four.

Mother's sister, Alma, born 1888;
very sweet when she wasn't crossed

According to her sisters, my Aunt Alma was sweet-natured when she wasn't crossed. But she carried within her chemistry the mortally wounded genes of her father, the Swashbuckler.

Uncle Albert said, "She just filled the bucket too full."

Alma graduated from high school as a real teacher's pet in 1905. Because she was intense and brilliant in every subject, and because her father had recently died in the insane asylum, the faculty at old Central High School in Toledo assembled a scholarship fund to help put her through Oberlin College.

After two years, when her funds ran out, she returned to Toledo to teach to earn extra money.

Then she went back to Oberlin with a passion and graduated in 1914 with both a bachelor's and a master's degree.

After graduation, a revealing odyssey began. She taught English literature and Shakespeare in Oak Park, Illinois; Bloomington, Indiana; Keyser, West Virginia; Arcadia and Santa Ana, California; and St. Cloud, Minnesota. Six cities in six years.

How could anyone, especially a woman in those days, change jobs so impetuously and so frequently? Travel so far? Find rooms? Make friends? Survive?

Poor wanderer, at the mercy of her genes (as aren't we all?). Aunt Iona said, "Alma would get angry about something, but she'd never argue." Instead of leaving the room, she'd leave the state.

Whenever Alma came home to visit, the family noticed how the ticking of a mantel clock seemed to annoy her so. She began to bewilder them with sudden suspicions and accusations. She thought people were lying to her and stealing from her.

Then, just like that, she was off to Europe with yesterday's flaming idealists, working for the League of Nations. In her words, "I believe in world peace to the last degree to bring out the best in the human spirit."

But dramatic personality changes startled her companions. The paranoia which had been dogging her finally overtook her in France. Much of a year was spent in the American hospital in Paris. Then the Red Cross put her on a boat for home.

Meanwhile Mama was remarried to a compassionate gentleman named Freeman May. Alone, he went to New York to meet Alma. On the train back to Toledo, Alma locked herself in a roomette, refusing to come out. The railroad telegraphed ahead, and Mama and Iona met the westbound train in Huron, Ohio, and finally lured Alma out by the time the train got to Toledo.

She came home a wreck, never to teach again.

Over the years she had been a talented and loving older sister, knitting an Oberlin sweater for her younger sister Edna's teddy bear, and exciting people by quoting Shakespeare.

But now she was annoying people at the courthouse, throwing clothes away when dirty, and ringing doorbells after midnight.

Her mother watched in dismay as she saw the same personality disorders in her daughter which had taken her husband to an early grave. Sorrowfully, she had Alma committed to the same asylum for the same reasons.

After six months of writing letters from the asylum, Alma was freed to the custody of Ruth Jones, a friend from St. Cloud. But soon another imagined offense and she was on the road again.

Poor wanderer.

She finally came to rest in Philadelphia, where the pacifist nature of her Quaker neighbors brought her some of the peace she sought.

The family understood at last that it was time to leave her alone. It was the only thing they could do.

She set up a little art studio on historic Elfreth's Alley where she "gave talks on Colonial history by candlelight and did artwork." The family was able, through friends or ministers, to get some money to her, and beyond that she was, like Blanche Dubois, "dependent on the kindness of strangers."

One July night in 1966 our phone rang, and a frail voice said, "Virginia, this is your Aunt Alma," just as if we'd been in touch all the time. I was moved by the sound of her fairy-tale voice.

Then began a flood of letters, sometimes deranged, often erudite and alive with her love of language, as she attempted to bizarrely reconnect with her lost family. But she chose to live out her disheveled life surrounded by ceiling-high stacks of her beloved books and jars of peanut butter, a near recluse, her reservoir of intellect virtually untapped.

Alas, poor Alma.

When I at last saw my intriguing aunt, it was too late. I stared in fascination at her closed eyes, looking for something I would never find.

Alas, poor me. For was she not my kindred spirit? Did she not love the same words I love?

Alma had finally come home to join her mama and papa and Chester in Woodlawn Cemetery.

ITINERANT GRANDMOTHER (Fifth Tale)

Alas, poor Mama.

By the time I was to know Mama (my *other* grandmother), she was in a state of suspended animation, as if she were waiting for some new shock to befall her.

The years had so eroded her "happy disposition" that I was never once to hear her sing or to see her dance in the way her daughters said "she used to."

By now she had lost her first husband to mental illness, her "baby" had drowned, her oldest daughter had "disappeared," and then her second husband, Mr. May, was killed in an automobile accident.

But there seemed to be no bitterness in her demeanor, just an aura of sorrow that I was too young to identify.

What remained of the original Mama was a pleasant nature, emptied of fire and emotion. It was as if she had used it all and had none left to expend. A certain life-force had gone from her, and all there was left for me to know was a quiet and enervated woman who listened patiently to my endless little-girl prattle when sometimes she slept with me on visits.

Itinerant grandmothers paid regular visits to lots of neighborhoods back in those unprotected days. With no Social Security and no pension plans to protect them, the widowed grandmothers were often cast adrift to become dependent on whichever of their children would take them in. And they slept uneasy in upstairs back bedrooms. Often they would finally die quietly in a loving daughter's home, but still wishing it could have been some other way.

I remember one nondescript day in late winter when I was seven or eight years old. I was very busy looking out the front window at nothing and very busy eating Pilgrim cookies. (The neat thing about Pilgrim cookies is that they had a hole in the center, and you could put the cookie on your index finger and eat round and round until you were left with nothing but a cookie ring.) I saw Grandma May getting off the Eleanor bus down at the corner. She exactly matched the forlorn day, creating a gray and wistful silhouette as she paused and waited for the bus to move on. Though I was glad to see her coming, I felt sad for her. She walked so slowly, with no enthusiasm. It was as if "she wouldn't know funny if it bit her in the underwear." My own mother's high-stepping enthusiasm was so unlike Grandma May's.

On those nights when Grandma slept with me, I would urge (pester) the poor woman to play endless word games in the cozy nighttime.

Me: I'm going to the store to buy something that begins with C.
Gr: Candy?
Me (disappointed): How did you know?
Gr (sleepily): I'm going to the store to buy something that begins with P.
Me: Plums? No. Pears? No. Peas? No. Peaches? No.

I continued questioning, as her voice drifted and grew hazy. "*Grandma!*"
She wakened long enough to mutter, "Pumpernickel."
Stopped cold, I lay in the darkness, impressed and quiet, listening to her steady breathing as I repeated the word "pum-per-nick-el" and made plans to use it against my next opponent in this rousing game.

UNCLE BOBBY, 1889–1951 (Sixth Tale)

Uncle Bobby was meant for better things.
But worse is what he got.
Lots worse.
When my father was born, Robbie, as the adults called him, was seven years old. When his new little brother was shown to him, Uncle Bobby is reported to have said, "Throw him in the alley!"
The information I have about Uncle Bobby makes it difficult to figure out what lay behind his troublesome behavior. Was his middle-child birth order responsible, or was his family status stolen by a talented, conscientious, amusing baby brother? Or was it simply in his genes?
Uncle Bobby always thought big. I'm talking *huge* when I tell you about the time he gave little Martha and little me each a root beer lollipop the size and shape of a flattened-out football. We worked on them through the entire fall and winter of 1933. Mother loved all-day suckers, but she knew an all-decade sucker when she saw one. So when spring came, she threw them out, and the tyranny ended.
We liked Uncle Bobby, and he liked us. Mother liked him too and even more so when he told her that her babies "always smelled so good."

As you know, he always thought big. What he got was small.

In the circle of yellow light which fell from the hanging green and gold Tiffany chandelier in Grandmother's dining room, the table was often covered with Uncle Bobby's papers and books and other trappings of his schemes.

I remember once he had a little printing press that printed advertising cards. While the ink was still wet, Uncle Bobby would let me sprinkle silver dust from a little bottle on the letters and make silver words. That's what he did. He sprinkled silver sometimes.

When he was still just a boy, we were told that he scandalized the family by becoming an habitué of pool halls.

Uncle Bobby, on the right, was already brooding in 1897. My father has the ringlets (!) on the left, and Albertha is in the center.

As he grew older, he walked along his predestined path in his pointy-toed shoes, making all the wrong moves, hanging out with all the wrong kids, drinking too soon and too much, and talking too big.

He married and divorced pretty dark-haired Elizabeth Stremmel, twice, and had no children.

When I was still young, and Uncle Bobby was still around, I used to watch him. I watched his pointy-toed shoes as he jiggled them and swung them back and forth and tapped them up and down during those restless, frustrated Sunday afternoonfuls of his chaotic dreams. Even as a kid I could sense the tension in him through his nervous feet.

He was in the room with us, but he wasn't really there at all.

And then slowly he began to disappear from family snapshots and portraits.

He began to disappear from the family.

Then he disappeared from the family home by court order because he had begun taking family heirlooms to sell for liquor.

We were to learn later that he began to hang out at the Rivoli Bar down at St. Clair and Cherry. When things got really bad for Uncle Bobby in the winter, he lived in a little room above the bar. Pete Arvanitis, who owned the bar, once said to me, "Your Uncle Bob knew books. He searched for rare ones and collected first editions, even at the Goodwill. Then he'd sell them in office buildigs downtown to educated people and probably people he'd known for years."

Bobby loved classical music and collected Caruso records. He'd sit in that dark little booth in that dark little bar in that down-at-the-heel neighborhood, with tears in his eyes, listening to the soaring, wrenching sounds of Pagliacci, who was saying it for Uncle Bobby, no doubt.

He cried a lot and said he couldn't go on.

Years later, Mr. Arvanitis said, "Your uncle started out a gentleman."

I knew nothing about this at the time it was happening.

On an October day in 1940, years after the last time I had seen my estranged uncle, two Toledo police officers walked up the wide front steps on Rosalind Place and told the weary, heard-it-all before, still-beautiful Julia that her first-born son had just zigzagged down the main street of Jackson, Michigan, and smashed into five cars.

I have pictured the scene on Rosalind in my mind many times. I see the wide, shaded front porch, the purposeful police, the knock on the big front door with the ornate brass handle, the frightened blue eyes, the hand moving quickly to rest at the throat, the stricken expression.

That very night, my weary, still-lovely grandmother Julia died of a heart attack. She died loving and forgiving her first-born, nice-guy-of-a-son, inexplicably gone wrong.

In May, 1951, when the world was all full of sun and promise for me, I sat on the front steps of Rosalind Place (then made into a duplex for young mothers Martha and me), holding my own "smelling-so-good" new son in my arms.

A few blocks away, and unknown to me, Uncle Bobby was walking out of the Lucas County Jail, due east on Jackson Street toward downtown Toledo. The night before he had turned himself in at the jail, appealing for help because he feared he was going to kill himself. He had tried and failed several days earlier in the old Navarre Hotel down near the Rivoli Bar. So the jail officers in their wisdom kept him overnight and released him the next morning, bandages still on his wrists, notifying no one.

Uncle Bobby walked slowly down Jackson, crossed Erie, Huron, Superior, St. Clair, and Summit streets. Then down the hill to Water Street and finally into the river that had been there all the time waiting for him. It took him sixty-two years. There he jumped in, taking in pointy-toed shoes and his guilt and his promise with him, to the family's second watery grave.

I remember when the movie *King Kong* was all the rage back in the thirties, Daddy said we absolutely couldn't go to see it. Uncle Bobby secretly took us to see the giant ape anyway.

Didn't I tell you he always thought big?

Uncle Bobby is in profile, with his hand on Martha's
arm and his ubiquitous straw hat in the other hand. I am
in front, on the left, with Julia, Mother, and Grandpa
behind me. Peggy is in the center.

I have felt haunted down the years because, after not having seen Bobby for ten years, I one day saw him downtown in the M&M Drug Store. Our eyes met for a long moment. I was now "Betty Coed." I could see that he was trying to superimpose the child I had been upon the college girl I now was. At a glance I saw my father's face beneath the brim of an old, stained hat, and a frayed polo coat with the collar turned up. I was leaving the drug store with a boyfriend, Bob Murphy, and I am forever ashamed that I just kept walking. I can still feel the yearning power of Uncle Bobby's stare.

Add this to my regret list. And then some.

Chapter 19

The world is run by people who don't love her very much.

—Howard Nemerov

- 'Twas the eighteenth of April in '75 (1775) when my paternal great-great-grandfather "marched on the alarm" at Lexington and Concord.
- In 1862, my maternal great-grandfather escaped from a Southern prison and returned north during the Civil War.
- In 1918, my father was gassed in the Ardennes in France in World War I.
- In 1944–45, my then future-husband coded top-secret American messages on a South Pacific atoll in World War II.
- In 1969–70, my collegiate son and his friends, "the Clean Gene Kids," resisted the Vietnam War.

My father rarely talked about World War I without choked-up patriotism in his voice. Each year on Memorial Day, or any day for that matter, a passing flag would render him momentarily speechless.

How could we kids have understood? It would take another whole war and another whole lifetime, and then we still couldn't grasp it all.

The grinding horror and destruction of my father's war, the trench warfare in France (1914–1918), that virtually tête-à-tête war, where thousands of young men per acre were killed, where no tree or other living thing was left standing, took up permanent residence in the psyches of the men who survived.

As a child, I listened halfheartedly to Daddy's rare wartime recollections. Although these recollections are lost forever, I do have sketches and photographs that Daddy left behind as a record of his brief encounter with man's major folly. It was an encounter that stayed with him and brought him close to tears off and on for all the rest of his life.

*Daddy got friendly with French peasant children;
he took this picture in 1919.*

DRILL ONLY LITTLE AND SLEEP A LOT

Corporal Mark Hannaford is a Toledo artist now in France with Company C. 114th Engineers. He writes to his friend, Victor La-Due of Toledo, that he is anxious to get back and reopen his studio in the Ohio building, now that the war is over. In a letter dated Dec. 26, Corp. Hannaford writes:

"We are still in this French camp, but are expecting to move

Mark Hannaford.

any day. Don't know when we will get home, but pray it will be within the next few months. This mud and rain are meant for frogs and web-feet, not for us. All we do is exercise a little, drill a little and sleep a lot. I am itching to get back into the game. I plan on staying at home for awhile and then hit it for Chi., and dig deep into the art stuff."

*Daddy was anxious to come home after the war;
he planned to "dig deep into the art stuff."*

PART TWO

The Depression era had been so demoralizing and fearful for our parents, but in 1941 they were to be filled with a new kind of fear, worse and different.

The fathers and mothers, who had so recently tenderly guided their little kids through the valley of the Depression, watched in agonizing dismay as their suddenly-tall young sons climbed onto trains and left for boot camp and for . . . Dear God, no . . . another war.

The parents waved good-bye in weeping wonder that it could possibly be happening again.

On a spring evening in 1943, Mother returned home unexpectedly early, after substituting in a neighborhood bridge club at Mrs. Campbell's house a few blocks west on Schuyler Road (over near the sunset).

Mother took a few quick steps into the living room, dropped into the Cogswell chair, and burst into tears. Baffled, Daddy and Martha and I closed into a natural circle around her as she babbled an explanation like a child would.

Sitting there in the flowered blue silk party dress, which she wore for years, she tremblingly told us that in the midst of the animated chatter and bridge mix at Mrs. Campbell's, the doorbell rang. Mrs. Campbell went to the door, and a Western Union messenger asked if she were Mrs. Campbell, and if she were alone. Like a blanket, silence dropped over the roomful of assembled maternal hearts.

The messenger handed the terrified mother of three sons a telegram.

Mrs. Campbell collapsed in screaming hysteria, sobbing over and over that her darling boy had been killed in action and was buried at sea. Don was her "favorite, . . . always had been," she wept. All those present and sorrowing with her, and for her, understood that at this most devastating of life's devastating moments, all lost children become their mother's favorites.

Mary Holton was a good high-school friend of mine. Together, we stepped over into the world of poetry, and we never came back. Mary had an older brother, Lloyd, who was some kind of god. I only saw him one time, standing in the late summer sun of 1942. Once was enough. Or it wasn't enough.

I never had seen such Great Gatsby-like good looks before, and I have seen few since. It was not a face one could forget. Before I could see him twice, he was off to Dartmouth and then fate intervened. I never saw him again.

Lloyd Holton, with his "Jay Gatsby good looks,"
didn't come home from the war.

The sad news came home with this wire.

As isolated and insulated young women, my friends and I were destined to live through a war in which fifty million people were killed, with only vague ideas of the immensity and horror of what was occurring every day around the world. We read about terrifying battles, which seemed somehow unreal, yet included boys with whom we had grown up.

Did we also serve? I hardly think so. It's hard to photograph what waiting looks like. At the University of Toledo, we did knit for, and write letters to, the far-flung boys. And we did without, emotionally. And we made the best of rationing and loneliness. We leaned on each other and built enduring alliances. We made the best of our lives in a one-sided world.

We managed to have a reasonable amount of involvement with young men because we dated air cadets who were stationed briefly at the university, or those who hadn't yet left for the service, or those who were exempt or home on leave. Some girls temporarily dropped out and got married, like Martha.

The rest of the time we had part-time jobs after classes, or we hung around the sorority apartment, laughing and talking, unaware that we were missing out on much of the intellectual and social exuberance that college life brings in normal times. We took trips together and read *The White Cliffs of Dover* together and cried together and sang "I'll Be Seeing You" and "The Last Time I Saw Paris" together.

Alice Weaver and I visited New York City in 1945, a week before FDR died. Here we are on top of the Empire State Building, before guardrails were installed on the observation deck.

We didn't really think about how the Depression had cheated our generation in one way, and now the war was cheating us in another. We were survivors.

Out of it all, we retained much of the joy of youth, even as we began to understand something of human loss and what it was like to feel helpless in a world on fire, in a world that needed help. We grew older and grew up and filled our memory banks with much blander memories than those of the young men with whom we would eventually spend our lives.

Chapter 20

One is always at home in one's past.

—Vladimir Nabokov

I think I will wonder off and on for the rest of my life about the kids on Overland Parkway, those first friends who grew up in those tidy wooden houses; those 1920 houses which faced each other, kept each other company, and provided shelter and solace through all the seasons of our growing. We grew up uniquely ourselves on the same plots of earth, under the same sun and moon, looking out of windows at the same scenery, and learning what to expect from the same neighbors, and walking the same exact steps past the same chicken pox and measles quarantine signs nailed on the same houses, and standing at the same penny candy counter at Yeager's across from Whittier School a zillion times.

The chorus of voices from the past often comes from other kids at Whittier, those I never saw or heard of again after time and strangers had carried us away into different worlds of our own.

Where are you, Lila Luther and Joy Seeman? I'm sorry you lost your mothers so soon. Where are you, Angelo Dovas? Did I ever thank you for that Valentine? And, Dick Dunham, you good-looking devil with the shy promise, are you okay? And Anna Whistler, with the fair skin and gold-rimmed glasses, are you still an old-fashioned girl? And Lois Gype? And Ted DeBoer? Are you out there somewhere? And the Johnson twins? And the Thompson twins? And Wilma Jacobs, are you still so blonde and cheerful? And pretty Betty Badman . . . and pleasant Dorothy Shough? Where are you now?

Looking back into the twenties and thirties through the doors of Whittier School, when the school was as new as the kids, is like looking at a prize-winning art film. Time has stopped there for me, caught in the sun slanting from above into the warm wooden halls, and in the light falling on the regimented toddlers marching in rows to the bathroom at designated times. And it lingers on the knickered, high-topped, barely under control boys and on the blooming, brand-new girls, and on the somber dresses of the teachers. It falls briefly on Miss Baer, the misunderstood, kindly principal who lived hidden under a Laugh-In hairnet and a Dickens persona.

The restrictive aura of the place matched the nailed-down furniture. But behind the classroom doors, the normal, high-spirited kids responded in kind to whichever teacher they had the good or bad luck to draw.

Miss Garfinkel, is it too late to tell you we're sorry about your crippled foot and matching personality? We're sorry that we were too young to understand your pain, and too young not to fear your gloomy glance as you hobbled down the hall in your medieval, high black shoes. It is too late for you to hear us.*

And Mr. Potter, janitor, sir, I remember that you fled the coal mines of Wales to come to America to clean the halls of Whittier School. I can still see your lean silhouette and your fine Welsh profile down the hall by Miss Tea's room, cleaning up where some little kid had thrown up. Was it better than the coal mines, though?

And amiable Miss Jane Smith, who taught second graders all about Japan because she had lived there for two years. Pretty soon we thought we had too. I recall the day when I fell down, and Miss Smith smothered me into her softly, coral-sweatered bosom. I still remember your warmth and your wit and your bosom. Years later Mrs. Molter told me that Jane Smith had said that she (Jane) didn't need a bra, she needed scaffolding. I like that one.

And pretty blonde third-grade teacher Miss Evelyn Thornberry, who sent a note home to Mother, "Watch Virginia's writing." It wasn't till much later that Mother learned that Miss Thornberry hadn't meant penmanship. Are you reading my book, Miss Thornberry?

And Miss Ames, who taught first grade in those little portable

---

*I learned one day recently that Miss Garfinkel escaped the Whittier schoolyard years ago, in a stream of verbal abuse from the children who feared her. She went to California for surgery on her foot and later committed suicide.

wooden classrooms which were quickly thrown together in a vacant field at the northern dead end of Overland Parkway in 1931. They were built to accommodate the flood of World War I babies who overflowed great big Whittier School.

Miss Ames, do you still have flaming bobbed hair, and do you still drive a lime green roadster with snap-on celluloid windows? That little chartreuse coupe of yours is overparked in my memory.

One day, Miss A., you looked up from your compact and caught me openly watching you put on makeup, and you made me stand in the corner till the bell rang. Why? Fifty years later I still don't get it. Maybe you were just a little kid yourself.

Whittier School still stands like Gibraltar, unaffected by all the snow and sun and rain and all the thousands of thundering young footsteps and all the years. It stands on Lewis Avenue near the Point in West Toledo. The Point was where four avenues—Lewis, Sylvania, Martha, and Phillips—flowed together to form a point and provide us with a prehistoric shopping center. There at the dime store I bought Mother her first Christmas pearls. And it was to the Point where I walked purposefully twelve blocks over and twelve blocks back for a thirty-cent Mother's Day geranium. The Point became my road to everywhere—to the library, the drug store, the doctor above the drug store, the Park Theatre, the dime store, Willys Park, my beat.

Every now and then I read on the obituary page about a Whittier classmate, and I am stunned by the loss of someone I haven't seen in forty or fifty years. I'm really only stunned of course to finally realize that, unlike Gibraltar, that old gang of mine and I are not indestructible after all.

Father Time is not always a hard parent, and though he tarries for none of his children, he often lays his hand lightly on those who use him well.

—Charles Dickens

Chapter 21

He was such a refreshing human being.

—Howard Remig
(a family friend)

I have lost the keys to many of the doors to those early days, but not the key to the bathroom on Overland Parkway where my earliest memory of my father places me in the bathtub.

The bathroom was a tiny pale blue room with a dark blue Indianlike design stenciled by Daddy along the walls above where the tile stopped. A leather razor strop hung from a white ceramic hook next to the washbowl.

I can almost remember what it feels like to be two and a half or three years old, standing in the tub with Daddy kneeling beside it. We are eyeballing each other and grinning as he draws a white towel (there weren't any colored towels then, as I recall) back and forth (as in shining shoes) across my small back to the beat of his song:

> *"Shine, shine,*
> *Shine 'em up fine,*
> *Shine 'em up fine*
> *For a dime."*

That's all, just a flashback, like in the movies. Just a flash, yet I retained enough of his caring that I sang the same song with my own children.

Daddy had a fine voice, and a song for everything:

(Flash) Bouncing us on his knee ("E-e-e-eemppp! i-i-i-iimppp! gimme piece o' pie-mppp!")

(Flash) Dancing while standing on Daddy's shoes ("Pony boy, pony boy, won't you be my honey boy?")

(Flash) Shooting us off the cannon of his feet (The "1812 Over-
ture")

(Flash) Carrying us to bed ("Fly away, Kentucky babe, fly away to
rest, fly away")

Daddy was a player of games, a singer of songs, and a trickster. He
made music with a spoon on his teeth, made his nose and his head
squeak, put a tiny rolled-up piece of paper in his ear and made it come
out his mouth, made his muscles do the Charleston, made a straight
pin disappear into the crook of his arm (I can do it myself), made
Peggy direct an orchestra, taught us to say "Lavator labia superiorus
ala canasi" 'cause it was the shortest muscle in the body with the
longest name (upper lip sneering muscle). He imitated the sound of
Tillotson's Model T starting up; he played "Heave, Ho! For the
Spanish Main!" nearly every time he passed the piano and made the
piano bench squeak along; and he said "Hush-a-mum-u-tut" when he
wanted us to be quiet; and he put his finger, with peanut butter on it,
in the dog's mouth and fell over backwards laughing; and told jokes
with ethnic accents that left us begging for more.

He called those he really liked a "peach" or a "prince" or a "brick,"
and those he didn't a "pup." When he wanted me to mind, I was "Lady
Jane." Many years later, when my parents were living in Florida and
we were visiting, Daddy came back from a little walk with my two-
year-old son, Richie, grinned at me and said, "That kid's a peach." I
knew he reserved that designation for a special few.

Instead of knighting people, he "peached" them!

The games and songs and tricks were interlaced with sensible,
down-to-earth assessments of the life going on around us, laughing,
coaxing, scolding, teasing me toward a vision of a world in which I
could laugh at myself. He was a pomp-puncturer.

If we said unkind things about anyone, he'd shorten an old Quaker
saying to "And even thou art a little queer." He said it often enough
that it finally became a family chorus that we'd all say at once when
one of us chose to criticize another. When we would bad-mouth
someone, say Peter Lorre or Fu Manchu or some other famous person,
Daddy'd say, "Why, he always said nice things about you."

He got angry and swore a lot (though he never said a dirty word),
and he sighed often. As we moved into adolescence, causing, I am
sure, a lot of increased sighing, I would, in the mindless way of
adolescents, sigh back at him sometimes.

Also, in those sheltered days, I never heard a dirty word at all, from any source. Little girls were protected much more back then. Once, on the school playground, when I was about twelve, I heard a boy say a strange word, "Bastard!" I knew it was a bad word because he was sitting on the other boy's chest and both their faces were scarlet.

Thirty years later, the grandson who had been peached when he was two years old, said of his long-gone grandfather: "My grandfather stands as one of those vanished spirits whom I knew very little and liked very much. He was wry, anxious, and boisterious, and a popular man. . . . He seemed, exactly as humorous as he was worried . . . as if anxiety and humor are rose and thorn from the same bush."

Despite his more boisterous side, Daddy was a gentleman, an utterly masculine man softened and molded by humor, a love of children and an inner sense of what really mattered. He was years ahead of his time in terms of his involvement with his children.

He carried a pocketknife—cutting string, peeling apples, sharpening pencils, solving endless small problems with his simple pocketknife. It irks me that my husband won't carry a little problem-solving knife.

Once, as Daddy chopped wood at a northern Michigan campsite in knee socks and corduroy knickers, his axe struck a petrified log. The axe flew back and nearly cut through his shinbone. Not trusting Mother to drive for help, since she had given up driving, he drove miles, bloody and bandaged, to the nearest town for a doctor. He was tough.

And he kneeled in our sunny-morning kitchen with a tiny, gold safety pin in his fingers and pinned a little lavender-checked hankie onto the yoke of my lavender-checked dress because I was crying before my first day of kindergarten.

"Now don't blow your nose on your dress," he teased.

I looked down at the little hankie, nearly camouflaged on my dress. Snuffling and giggling, I looked at his tender smile, blurred and glistening through my arrested tears, and I loved him so. He could take the pain away like cool water on a burn. And there were rules. We weren't spoiled. He was a father who said *no* and he meant *no:*

1. *No* to junk food at the circus.
2. *No* to going to the mortuary to see Elizabeth Johnson, my little second-grade classmate who had died in October, 1932 of pneumonia and was buried in her Halloween costume.
3. *No* to seeing the movie *King Kong.* (Uncle Bobby took us secretly.)

4. *No* to gossip.
5. *No* to seeing a two-headed baby at the Chicago World's Fair in 1933. (*Not* fair).
6. *No* to pretense.

And he said yes a lot more than he said no.

He was a barbershop singer and a joiner. He belonged to the American Legion and the Exchange Club, High Twelve, the Toledo Artists' Club, and the Art Klan.

He turned down the more prestigious Tile Club because he thought it would cost too much, and prestige didn't mean that much to him.

The Art Klan, Toledo's oldest art organization, met every Thursday night for drawing or painting from a costumed model or a female nude. Daddy never missed. One Thursday night, as Mother made plans as usual to get together with her friend Luella LaDue and her two cute, rambunctious boys, Bob and Dick (the same ages as Martha and I), she sighed as Daddy walked through the dining room with his familiar big box of pastels. "Well, Mark," she said, "If you don't know how to draw the female body by now, you never will."

I want to tell you a story which involves Daddy and the Fourth of July, circa 1933.

We measured our lives in holidays then. I suspect we still do. The holiday which has changed the most, and which I miss the most, is the Fourth of July. We all know that fireworks need to be illegal, but nothing can stop the rush of memory when we waken even now on the morning of the Fourth.

Back in the thirties the neighborhood kids were always up and out early, into the sweet freshness of a morning smelling of leftover June roses and gunpowder. There's nothing like it. We'd sit on the cool sidewalk and compare our limited arsenals of sparklers and snakes and tiny red firecrackers. Most of us weren't allowed the risky things like torpedoes and cherry bombs and three-inch salutes.

At night Daddy would nail a pinwheel to the maple tree out in front, and as it fiercely whirled, spitting showers of colored sparks, we'd all scream. Then someone's father would touch the punk to a fountain, which would spew volcanically into the air, and we'd scream again. That was it, unless we went out to see the city's fireworks at Walbridge Park on the Maumee and sat on the terraced bank and got all mixed up in the fireworks and the stars and the tens of thousands of people.

The neighborhood dogs, despite our ineffective attempts at consolation, spent the following week under a bed.

Just before the Fourth in 1933 or 1934, Mother was briefly in the hospital, and Daddy was nervous squared.

Somehow, Martha had gotten ahold of one of those forbidden little torpedoes. Torpedoes were and are the size of a jawbreaker, but when they're hurled to the sidewalk, they become a miniature bomb. On this particular sunny noontime, Daddy was hurrying in the back door, carrying two sackfuls of groceries. I was in the kitchen in my bathing suit, waiting for my afternoon frolic in the sprinkler. Martha, age ten or eleven, in a fit of uncharacteristic devilment, crept up behind Daddy, just outside the door, and hurled the torpedo to the sidewalk.

First, Daddy lost control of the groceries. Then, he lost control of his temper. Then Peggy lost control of her bladder and ran around in circles barking. I stepped to one side, agog at my sister. Martha looked on dumbfounded at what she had wrought. Daddy made tracks up the four steps into the kitchen to the bottle of nerve medicine on the kitchen counter which he took without benefit of spoon.

Martha went back to her old ways after that.

Daddy had a fault which loomed large among his many good qualities. It made a regular annual appearance every September nineteenth on Mother's birthday. It involved a two-pound box of Fanny Farmer chocolates. Every year she got that same thing for her birthday from Daddy, and every year she was hoping for something better or something different. One particular September nineteenth, I was sitting nearby as Mother stood at the front screen door, looking idly out into the warm and windy afternoon. She happened to see Daddy getting off the bus with the telltale white box under his arm. She cut her eyes over at me, her eyebrows raised, and said, "Guess what? Candy for my birthday."

I hadn't realized. Daddy stepped in the door proudly and handed her the box (half filled, I was to learn, with candies she couldn't stand), as if it were a wonderful surprise. I watched how she handled her disappointment. She tried. She smiled as she always did, hesitated and then, unable to stand it for another year, muttered, "The least you could do is get all maple walnuts."

Daddy looked surprised and crestfallen. I don't think he had any idea. This imaginative man had no imagination when it came to gifts costing more than two dollars and ninety-eight cents. I don't remember her ever getting anything very special in the way of gifts. They were both Depression casualties in that sense.

There was a night in summer, perhaps 1936, when Daddy and Mr. Lennex took Pinkie and me (ages eleven and twelve) down to the Franklin Ice Cream store on Sylvania Avenue for extravagant banana splits (twenty-five cents each).

The waitress brought the bill, and I realized in a flush of embarrassment that Daddy made no move to pick it up. In a swift and natural gesture, Mr. Lennex said the treat was on him. No resistance from Daddy.

Then I remembered all those times that Daddy had sighed over this expenditure, or that. He'd say, "Don't you think there's any bottom to my pocket?" Mother would say, "Don't tell your father yet about your new sweater," and he'd say "Don't you think there's any tomorrow?" when we'd eat too much of something.

I began to resent this. A lot.

Then one day in 1944 (when I was twenty), I threw caution to the wind and said, "Daddy, could I have one hundred dollars (it seemed like a thousand then) to go visit Alice at Swarthmore?" Without a blink he said yes, and I knew that the Depression was indeed over, and that when he had more, he gave more. The flaw which I had resented was simply fear, and it was a fear that followed my father's life to the very end.

And Mother grew old, dreaming nightly that she had lost her purse.

By now, Martha and I had begun dating a lot. When we finally got past having to get Mother's approval for each date, she switched to "Who do you have a date with tonight?"

Then, "Oh, *his* mother is such a snob."

Next date, "Oh, *his* mother is so odd."

Or, "You know your father doesn't want you to go out with Catholic boys or Jewish or Italian or or or." But once we became interested in a boy, Mother was usually pleasant and fun. Her basic nature was generous and caring.

Daddy took that period of our lives pretty much in stride, joking easily with each young man, teasing him about his football beard ("first down") and, when his trousers were baggy at the knees, which they often were, he'd ask, "When are you going to jump?" And everyone would die laughing, and no one would seem to mind, especially the boy who enjoyed the offhand intimacy.

As a child, sometimes I'd lie in bed and look down the short upstairs hall to the bathroom where my father would be standing in his BVDs (Button all the vay down, he said), swishing his straight razor up and down on the razor strop.

I watched him as a child watches, soaking up the details of his face, his ruddy complexion, his mustache, his tousled hair, his posture, his behavior, not knowing that I was soaking them up forever.

He'd lean toward the mirror and begin to shave, his muscular legs bowed back behind the knee (like mine). He would hum as he shaved, and his muscular body would sway ever so slightly to the sound of its own music.

When he was around—shaving, mowing, cooking, dancing, digging, drawing, singing—all seemed right with the world.

I watched him down that hall till his hair turned white.

My last memory of the upstairs hall is a cool, rainy morning in June of 1944. Daddy came into my bedroom and wakened me by dabbing lather from his shaving brush on the end of my nose. He wanted to tell me that the invasion of Normandy had just begun. His face looked sad and older. Perhaps he was remembering an earlier war in France, in the Ardennes, the mustard gas, the shell shock, the fear, the lasting trauma.

It was the end and the beginning of lots of things.

We moved away from Overland Parkway that summer, but I kept an imaginary key to the front door. It was the only one I needed.

Now, the Fourths of July and the torpedoes and the Halloweens and burning living room lamps and the Christmasses and the tender moments and the disappointments and the exploding innertubes and the asthmatic nights and the summer vacations and the promising kids and the comforting pets and the blooming gardens and the high hopes and the little girls grown big and the moment upon moment wonders were gathering speed. The future was hurtling toward us.

The neurotic dread of poverty, which claimed so many of that generation's parents, never quite let go of Daddy, but still he had his art and his "Eddie" and his girls. He and Mother clung to their early "great expectations" and seemed contented as time started to intrude. Despite the fact that they never got rich, they must have felt they'd made it, for there was never the least hint of abandoned hope in their natures.

Mother and Daddy at my wedding, January 10, 1948

December, 1962. Florida.

As I reluctantly and tearfully approached Daddy's coffin with Mother, she leaned over and put her hand over his.

She was quiet for a long time as she studied his face.

"Your father had no vanity," she said finally.

He was a peach, I thought.

Then we fell apart.

All that cold winter long it seemed as if something were wrong, as if I'd left a door open somewhere in the house, and an icy draft was coming in. That's what the world seemed like without him.

Daddy remained quotable. His voice echoes down the years to me: "You get back exactly what you give in this world, little girl."

And Mother's too: "Never put a lid on warm chicken, Gin."

Epilogue

The last thing we learn is what comes first.

—Howard Nemerov

In the beginning on Overland Parkway, there had been such an endless vista stretching ahead . . . of days to burn, days to waste, days to dream in, plan in, grow in. Time swam about in the rooms, and we kids played and learned and laughed and cried and ate and dreamed and pouted and slept and thought about ourselves nonstop.

We knew what we wanted, and we wanted something every minute. Then, in no time, we didn't know what we wanted at all. And then we did.

We'd look in the mirror at the reflection we knew and loved so well, and sometimes we'd wonder who we would have been if our mother had married some strange guy, and for one moment we'd feel very odd.

Despite the economic woes that engulfed the country and our parents, the years were still full of bright promise because there were children growing up. The children were the carriers of the genes and dreams of their family's heritage.

And then at last our generation grew up and found someone to love and marry. For me, it was Dick, who was funny and wise and sensitive and anxious. Together we were caught up in the universal wonder of children of our own.

For us, it was Richie and Sarah.

We stopped thinking about ourselves and watched in amazement the magical mystery tour of our children's growth. Our hearts flew back in time, again and again, as we understood with growing gratitude what our own parents had done for us and felt for us . . .

what all the generations before us had done and felt, each in its imperfect turn. Now it was our turn.

At last, we knew the meaning of it all.

Now, that limitless, long-ago vista of days is stretched out behind me, and I am left with none to spare, none to burn. Each day needs to count. I live now in a world I once could not imagine, a world without parents and a world with children and grandchildren of my own who live far away on either coast.

They come to visit, Mother and Daddy and the kids.

When Daddy comes, he is always wearing corduroy knickers and knee socks, and he is young. He carries a garden spade and a watercolor brush, and he tells me wise and funny things.

If he had known he would one day walk into an endless future with me in his old brown knickerbockers, he would have thrown back his head and laughed.

Sometimes I put on his rimless glasses and look to see if I can find him in the mirror.

Mother always comes to see me in her white and green eyelet dress, with her hair dark and marcelled in perfect waves against her cheeks. She loses no time as she chats, sprinkling, cooking, sewing, ironing, touching my hair as she passes.

She sashays into her endless future with me, cheerful, guileless, and unafraid.

Not a day goes by that their flickering images don't come into focus for me.

For Daddy, I go back into the house to turn out the lights so I don't leave "so much hell burning." For him, I peel the potatoes closer.

For Mother, I tidy up the living room before I go to bed so I "won't have to face it in the morning." For her, I tie a perfect bow.

For them, I am myself.

Richie and Sarah, now grown into funny, wise, humane and, sometimes, anxious adults, come back from New York and Idaho in planes and trains and cars. Sometimes they come back as toddlers in my dreams.

I am refreshed always by the precise, fresh, naive language of children. In my dreams, Richie at three asks me again, "Mommy, who blows the wind?" At fifteen, he says in the darkness, "Mom, I need a psychiatrist because I need to know everything *now*."

At four, Sarah orders, "Tiptoe as hard as you can, Mommy." At ten, she reports, "I want to be a chemist some day because I love explosions."

In airports and train stations near and far we scan the torrents of strangers, and lo! and suddenly, there they are, tall and blue-eyed, looking over the crowd—their once marshmallow cheeks lean and flushed with anticipation.

Richie and his wife, Mary, and their two little girls, Elizabeth and Rebecca; and Sarah and her husband, Frank, emerge from the torrent. The crowd evaporates, and we are alone in a hugging circle.

Then, across a void of mystery, vanished family members crowd into the circle, and we, each in our own private way, are touched by the fiction for a moment. Somehow, we all know that in the hugging circle lies the future.

We are again, and for a little while, one family, under God, indivisible, with liberty and justice and humor and love and charity and memories for all.

Index